Cambridge English

Complete IELTS

Bands 6.5–7.5

Teacher's Book

**Guy Brook-Hart and Vanessa Jakeman
with David Jay**

CAMBRIDGE
UNIVERSITY PRESS

University Printing House, Cambridge CB2 8BS, United Kingdom

Cambridge University Press is part of the University of Cambridge.

It furthers the University's mission by disseminating knowledge in the pursuit of education, learning and research at the highest international levels of excellence.

www.cambridge.org
Information on this title: www.cambridge.org/9781107609648

© Cambridge University Press 2013

First published 2013

A catalogue record for this publication is available from the British Library

ISBN 978-1-107-62508-2 Student's Book with Answers with CD-ROM
ISBN 978-1-107-65760-1 Student's Book without Answers with CD-ROM
ISBN 978-1-107-64281-2 Class Audio CDs (2)
ISBN 978-1-107-60964-8 Teacher's Book
ISBN 978-1-107-63438-1 Workbook with Answers with Audio CD
ISBN 978-1-107-66444-9 Workbook without Answers with Audio CD
ISBN 978-1-107-68863-6 Student's Pack (Student's Book with Answers with CD-ROM and Class Audio CDs (2))

Contents

Introduction

Who *Complete IELTS* is for

Complete IELTS is an enjoyable and motivating topic-based course designed to give thorough preparation for the IELTS test. It offers:

- comprehensive analysis and practice of the **task types** used in IELTS Reading, Listening, Speaking and Writing papers
- a step-by-step approach to **writing tasks** using models as guidance and sample answers
- a systematic approach to **speaking tasks** with model answers and a focus on pronunciation
- stimulating authentic reading texts that provide training in the skills and strategies needed to deal with exam **reading tasks**
- listening activities that provide training in the skills and strategies needed to deal with exam **listening tasks**
- coverage of major **grammar** and **vocabulary** areas which are known to be essential for success in IELTS. These are supported by work on correcting common mistakes as revealed in the Cambridge Learner Corpus
- motivating **pair work** and **group work** exercises.

What the Student's Book contains

- **Eight topic-based units of ten pages** each covering topic areas frequently encountered in IELTS.
- Each unit covers tasks from each of the four papers in the exam, so all units contain work on **Listening, Reading, Writing** and **Speaking**. The units also cover **essential IELTS-related grammar and vocabulary**.
- Each exam task type is integrated into a range of classroom activities designed to equip students with the **strategies and approaches** needed to deal with the demands of IELTS.
- Practice for each part of the test is accompanied by **detailed information and advice** about what the task involves and how best to approach it.
- **Eight unit reviews** that provide additional exercises on the grammar and vocabulary encountered in each unit.

- **Writing** and **Speaking reference sections** containing detailed advice to students on how to approach writing and speaking tasks in the exam, complete with exercises and model answers.
- A **Language reference section** giving clear and detailed explanations of the grammar covered in each unit.
- A **full IELTS Practice test**.
- A **CD-ROM intended for self-study** which provides further exercises to prepare students for IELTS.

The Cambridge Learner Corpus (CLC) ⊘

The Cambridge Learner Corpus (CLC) is a large collection of exam scripts written by students taking Cambridge ESOL English exams around the world. It contains over 220,000 scripts and is growing all the time. It forms part of the Cambridge International Corpus (CIC) and it has been built up by Cambridge University Press and Cambridge ESOL. The CLC contains scripts from:

- 200,000 students
- 170 different first languages
- 200 different countries.

Exercises in the Student's Book which are based on the CLC are indicated by this icon ⊘.

What the Workbook contains

- **Eight units designed for homework and self-study.** Each unit contains full exam practice of **IELTS Reading** and **Listening tasks**.
- **IELTS Writing tasks** with model answers.
- Further practice of the **grammar** and **vocabulary** taught in the Student's Book.
- An **audio CD** containing all the listening material for the Workbook.

What the Teacher's Book contains

- **Detailed notes** for the eight units in the Student's Book which:
  - state the **objectives** of each unit

- give **step-by-step advice** on how to treat each part of each Student's Book unit
- give **supporting information** to teachers and students about IELTS tasks
- offer suggestions for **alternative treatments** of the materials in the Student's Book
- offer a wide range of ideas for **extension activities** to follow up Student's Book activities
- contain **comprehensive answer keys** for each activity and exercise, including suggested answers where appropriate.

• **Eight photocopiable activities**, one for each unit, designed to provide enjoyable recycling of work done in the Student's Book unit, but without a specific exam focus. All photocopiable activities are accompanied by teacher's notes outlining:
- the objectives of the activity
- a suggested procedure for handling the activity in the classroom.

• **Eight photocopiable Word lists** containing lexical items encountered in the Student's Book units or recording scripts.

We suggest that the best time to use these lists is towards the end of the unit, perhaps before doing the Speaking or Writing sections. Students may use these lists for self-study and reinforcement of lexis encountered in the unit. Here are some suggestions as to how students can use them which you can discuss with them.

- Students should use the page reference given to find the items in the unit and study how the words/phrases are used in context.
- They can use a learner's dictionary (such as the *CALD*) to compare the dictionary definitions with the definitions given in the Word list. In many cases, the definitions will coincide, but they will be able to study further examples in the dictionary.
- Students can annotate the Word lists themselves or copy items to their notebooks for further study.
- You can suggest to students that they should not try to memorise all the items, but they should select a number of words and phrases that seem most useful

to them and try to use them when doing speaking and writing tasks.

• **Eight photocopiable Vocabulary extension word lists**

The words and phrases in the photocopiable Vocabulary extension word lists have been selected using the Cambridge International Corpus and relate to the topics of the unit. They are intended to provide students with extra vocabulary when doing IELTS tasks.

We suggest that you hand these lists out near the beginning of the unit. Most of the words and phrases do not occur in the units themselves, but students may be able to use some of them during the speaking or writing activities in the unit. Here are some suggestions on how these word lists can be used:

- Ask students to go through the word lists in conjunction with a good learner's dictionary such as the *CALD* and check how the words/phrases are used in the examples (many of the definitions will be the same).
- Ask students to select 5–10 items which they would like to be able to use themselves and ask them to write their own sentences using the items.
- Encourage students to copy the items they find most useful to their notebooks.
- Ask students to refer to these word lists before doing speaking or writing tasks in the units. Give students time to look at the relevant list and think (and discuss with you) how they can use words/phrases before they do the task itself.
- When students do the tasks, pay particular attention to any use they make of items from the lists and give them feedback on how correctly they have used an item.

• **Four photocopiable Progress tests**, one for every two units, to test grammar and vocabulary taught in the units.

What the Class Audio CDs contain

There are **two audio CDs** containing **listening and speaking material** for the eight units of the Student's Book plus the Listening Practice test. The listening and speaking materials are indicated by different-coloured icons for each of the CDs.

Unit 1 Getting higher qualifications

Unit objectives

- **Listening Section 1:** introduction to form completion; identifying what information is needed
- **Vocabulary:** dependent prepositions
- **Reading Section 1:** introduction to skimming and scanning; recognising references; 'True / False / Not Given', note completion and short-answer question tasks
- **Speaking Part 1:** using higher-level vocabulary; talking about past habits and states
- **Pronunciation:** sentence stress 1 – stressing important words that answer questions
- **Writing Task 1:** rephrasing information in the task using your own words; writing the introductory sentence; analysing graphs and describing the main features; paragraphing, organising and structuring an answer
- **Key grammar:** past simple, present perfect simple and past perfect simple

Starting off

❶ *As a warmer* Write these questions on the board and ask students to discuss them in small groups with books closed.
- *Why are you preparing for the IELTS test?*
- *What personal qualities help people to be successful at language exams?*

If you wish, round up with the whole class and turn it into a general class discussion.
- With books open, ask students to look at the example and say whether it is a definition or an example (*answer:* an example).
  Alternative treatment Ask students to look at the example in the book. Then ask them to work in pairs and hand each pair a piece of paper with one of the other personal qualities (b–h) written on it.
- Ask students to look at the other qualities (b–h) and write down what it means to have that quality, without naming it.
- When students are ready, they read out what they have written to the whole class. The class then says which quality they are describing and discusses how accurate they think the description is.
- When they have finished, ask students to compare their answers with the suggested answers on page 96.

Suggested answers
a You do things like read documents very carefully and focus on all the small points, checking their accuracy.
b You are able to think about something and come up with an original or unusual approach to it.
c When you come across something new, you are eager to learn or find out about it.
d You are able and willing to work with other people as part of a group in order, for example, to solve problems or develop new ideas.
e You can look ahead and plan how an organisation or company might best meet the needs of the future.
f You are friendly and energetic, and find it easy and enjoyable to be with others.
g You find it easy to exchange ideas with others; you listen well and can accurately put across your own ideas.
h You can look after and organise groups of employees so that they are performing in the best interests of the company.

❷ Tell students to give reasons for their answers.

Suggested answers
1 a, c   2 f, g, h   3 d, g, h   4 a, c   5 a, b, e   6 f, g

Extension idea Ask students to choose two of the photos and say what other personal qualities the people need (apart from a–h).

❸ Tell students that, in the Speaking test, they will usually be expected to give quite long answers, backing up their opinions by giving reasons.

Extension idea Ask students to say what qualities they personally already have.

Listening Section 1

❶ *As a warmer* With books closed, ask students to discuss in small groups (you can write the questions on the board):
- *How can students in your country find out about careers and jobs?*
- *How do young people in your country decide what job they would like to do?*
- *What did you decide to study, and why?*

- If any of them mention graduate recruitment fairs, use this as a stepping stone to the questions in the book. If they do not, write the term on the board and ask them what they understand by it.
- Focus students on the three questions in the book and ask them to discuss the questions in pairs.
- When students have finished, particularly if you are teaching a multicultural class, round up with the whole class.

> **Suggested answers**
> 1 People from different companies advertise for new staff. / Displays attract candidates. / Candidates seek out job opportunities. They provide an opportunity for graduates to meet directly with potential employers.
> 2 There are fewer jobs, so greater competition for each job. Vocational training may be more useful, as there are now more students with degrees, and vocational qualifications may be a more reliable assessment of skills and competencies for practical jobs where experience counts.
> 3 experience in the field / other positions of responsibility / engagement at interview

Extension idea Ask students: *Do you have graduate fairs in your country? Have you ever been to one? What was it like?*

❷ • Draw students' attention to the Exam information on page 9. Point out that, in the IELTS test, they hear each section once only, so it is important to know what to expect before listening. Also mention that they need to write their answers in the question booklet while the recording is playing; they have ten minutes to transfer them onto an answer sheet at the end of the test. This means they can underline things in the question booklet as they do the test, but they need to make sure they can read their answers later on.
- Refer students to the point about the increasing difficulty of the test. At this level, they should find Section 1 easy and they should be able to get close to full marks.
- Form-completion tasks test students' ability to listen for specific details. It is important for students to know what details they should listen for beforehand.
- Tell students that Section 1 nearly always includes a form or table to complete. In the exam, they will have a short time (about 15 seconds) to read the questions and decide what information they need. Their performance will improve if they know what information they should be listening for before they start.

- Draw students' attention to the instructions in Questions 1–10. Tell them that the instructions will always clearly state how many words they can write, (e.g. *ONE WORD / NO MORE THAN TWO/ THREE WORDS AND/OR A NUMBER*), so it is important to always check before they start. If the instructions state ONE WORD, but they write two, they will not get any marks for that question.
- Ask students to discuss what information they need in pairs.

> **Suggested answers**
> 1 a surname / family name that may be spelled out
> 2 a nationality
> 3 an email address that may be spelled out
> 4 a type of BA
> 5 a date
> 6 an activity or event which might raise money
> 7 some interests
> 8 names of job(s)
> 9 the name of a job
> 10 how they heard about the fair

Extension idea Tell students that, in Section 1, they will usually have to write a name that is spelled out for them and/or write a number. Ask them which questions might require this (*answer*: Questions 1 and 3).
- Ask them if there are any letters or symbols which they are not sure how to pronounce in English and resolve any doubts.
- Ask them to write two or three names and email addresses on a piece of paper, and then spell them aloud to their partners, who should write them down.

❸ 🎧 *Alternative treatment* Although in the exam each section is heard only once, you can play the recording a second time for students to check their answers.

- Draw their attention to Question 7, where they need two interests. Tell them that if they only write one, they will not get the mark.
- Tell them that sometimes words can be added or omitted without penalty (see words in brackets in the answer key).

> **Answers**
> 1 Alexandrovna
> 2 (She is) Russian
> 3 dom54
> 4 (a) full-time
> 5 21st July / 21/7 / 21 July / July 21 / July 21st / 7/21
> 6 competition
> 7 cooking/cookery; swimming (*must have both*)
> 8 (a) children's tutor
> 9 (a) project manager
> 10 (a) friend

Extension idea Go through the Exam advice box with students.
- Stress that correct spelling is essential and that they should check it when they transfer their answers to the answer sheet.
- Elicit some common abbreviations (you can ask students to write these on the board), e.g. *kilometres* (*km*); *seconds* (*secs*); *minutes* (*mins/min*); *hours* (*hrs/ hr*); *Jan, Feb*, etc.; *Mon, Tues*, etc.
- Tell students that if they are not sure how to write the abbreviations correctly, they should write them in full.

❹ Tell students that they are quite likely to be asked about the topics in this exercise in Part 1 of the Speaking test, so it is a good idea to have some ideas and vocabulary to describe themselves before the exam. Give students a few minutes to think about what they want to say and how to express it before they start. Where necessary, help them with vocabulary.

Alternative treatment You can ask students to do this exercise after they have done the vocabulary section which follows. In this way, they will have an opportunity to practise the vocabulary and prepositions.

Vocabulary Dependent prepositions

❶ Wrong choice of preposition is a major area of error for IELTS candidates at this level.

As a warmer Write on the board:
- *He wasn't aware ...... the time.*
- *How do you prepare ...... exams?*
- Ask students to say what preposition should go in each gap (*aware of, prepare for*). Write *get ready* and *conscious* and ask them what preposition follows each (*get ready for, conscious of*). Point out that words with similar meanings often (but not always) have the same preposition, so this is a good way of guessing when they are not sure which preposition to write. Other examples you can give or elicit: *afraid of, frightened of, scared of; angry with, irritated with, annoyed with*.

Answers
1 to **2** of/in/with **3** on
4 for **5** at **6** to/for/in

Extension idea Check that students know the correct dependent preposition for each word, then ask them to think of synonyms that use the same preposition: *concentrate (focus on); available (free for); useful (essential/vital/important for).*

❷ Before doing this exercise, briefly refer students to the Language reference (page 112).
- Tell them that the words and dependent prepositions in this section are generally useful in IELTS exams.
- Tell them to do the exercise and then check their answers in the Language reference.

Answers
1 on **2** to **3** for **4** in **5** in **6** of

Extension idea Tell students that, in IELTS, it is important to use a range of vocabulary appropriately. Working with words with similar or synonymous meanings helps to build vocabulary.
Write these words on the board and ask students to find words in the exercise which are close in meaning to them (though not all synonyms) and to decide if they need to change the preposition or not.
is known   keep an eye   responsive   take part   trust
(*answers:* is known *for* / has a reputation *for*; keep an eye *on* / take care *of*; responsive *to* / sensitive *to*; take part *in* / participate *in*; trust *in* / have confidence *in*.)

❸ Point out to students that they have to learn dependent prepositions with the words themselves, so it may be worth them studying lists such as the ones in the Language reference. Again, when they have finished the exercise, ask them to use the Language reference to check their answers.

Answers
2 ~~with~~ for **3** ~~into~~ in **4** ~~students the~~ students with the **5** ~~responsible to~~ responsible for **6** ~~on~~ to
7 ~~deal many~~ deal with many

Reading Section 1

❶ ***As a warmer*** Ask students to work in small groups and look at the Exam information, particularly the last bullet.
- Ask them to suggest ways they can control their time and make sure they have enough time for the whole paper.
- When they have finished, round up with the whole class. (Suggestions they may come up with: spend less time on Section 1 so as to leave more time for the more difficult sections; do the more difficult sections first; put their watch on the table and keep a strict control over their time.) The important point is that they should realise that time management is essential to success in the exam.
- Tell them that they will be practising different reading techniques while doing this section in the book, so doing the section in class will take longer than the maximum 20 minutes they would spend in the exam.

- Before they do the exercise in the book, elicit that *prestigious* means 'it has a good reputation'.

Suggested answers
2 higher than average results / strong leadership / long history / ground-breaking research / good teaching
3 their degree may be worth more / it may help them get a better job / it gives them prestige / they get better teaching

❷ **Answers**
1 **a** Scanning **b** Skimming
2 You can scan for a key word/phrase in a question to quickly find the place where the answer is.
   You can skim parts of the passage to understand the key ideas and quickly match these to questions or statements.

❸ Before students read, elicit the meaning of *skim*.
- Explain that it is important to skim the passage to get a general idea of the contents before reading it more carefully. If they do this, they will find it easier to locate the answers to questions, deal with tasks and so save time as they work through the section.
- Tell students that they should not try to understand every word and every sentence; give them three minutes to skim the passage. Be strict with the time limit.

Answer
b

❹ Tell students that finding the answers to questions often requires them to understand two or three linked sentences of text, and that writers use referencing techniques to link sentences together.
- To illustrate the point, you can write on the board: *There has been a rapid expansion of the university system. This has meant that many more young people are attending such institutions, and the result of this is that the labour market is being deprived of their services until later.*
- Ask students to point out the referencing devices and say what they refer to (*answers: this* refers to the rapid expansion of the university system; *such institutions* refers to universities; *the result of this* refers to more young people attending university; *their services* refers to the services of young people).
- Elicit the meaning of *scan*.

Answers
2 *to leap into the dark and reach for the unknown*
3 *The telephone, electromagnets, radars, high-speed photography, office photocopiers, cancer treatments, pocket calculators, computers, the Internet, the decoding of the human genome, lasers, space travel*
4 *Knowledge was at a premium, but it had to be useful.* (also *the German system of learning based on reseach and hands-on experimentation*)
5 *symbiosis* refers to the motto *Mind and hand* and the logo showing *a gowned scholar standing beside an ironmonger bearing a hammer and anvil.*
6 *he might be just too late in taking his concept to market, as he has heard that a Silicon Valley firm is already developing something similar.*
7 *What MIT delights in is taking brilliant minds from around the world in vastly diverse disciplines and putting them together.*

❺ True / False / Not Given (TFNG) tasks test whether candidates can correctly identify information is expressed in the text or not.

Tell students that the TFNG task is often found in Reading Section 1.
- Tell them that the questions in TFNG tasks usually contain one or two words, e.g. *MIT campus*, which are the same as or similar to a word or phrase in the passage. This is to help them locate the part of the passage which relates to the statement.
- Point out that, since they skimmed the passage earlier, locating this information should be quicker and that it may not be necessary at any stage to read the whole passage slowly and in detail to answer the questions. The key words, in effect, serve as a short cut to the relevant parts of the passage, and students should scan until they find these.
- Tell students that proper names (e.g. *MIT, Silicon Valley*) in the questions are almost always going to serve as key words, since they cannot be paraphrased and are therefore easy to scan for in the passage.

Suggested underlining
2 **2** Harvard / MIT **3** motto / MIT student **4** logo **5** Silicon Valley

6 Before students answer the questions, draw their attention to the Exam advice. Tell them that it is often difficult to decide if a question is False or Not Given. Students should choose False when the information in the passage **contradicts** the statement. They should choose Not Given when there is **no information** about the statement in the passage.

Extension idea Ask students to work in pairs and compare their answers. Ask them to quote the actual words from the passage which gave them their answers.

Answers
1 FALSE (*… there's precious little going on that you would normally see on a university campus.*)
2 FALSE (*While Harvard stuck to the English model of a classical education, with its emphasis on Latin and Greek, MIT looked to the German system of learning based on research and hands-on experimentation.*)
3 NOT GIVEN (The motto is mentioned, but we are not told who suggested it.)
4 TRUE (*… its logo, which shows a gowned scholar standing beside an ironmonger bearing a hammer and anvil. That symbiosis of intellect and craftsmanship …*)
5 NOT GIVEN (There is nothing in the text about how much MIT graduates are paid in Silicon Valley.)

7 Note-completion tasks test students' abilities to scan the passage for specific information. They reflect the type of reading activity that might be required on an undergraduate course of study. The instructions will tell students how many words they can use for each gap.

Before students do the task, draw their attention to the Exam advice box.
- Point out that by reading the title and scanning to find the right part of the passage, they can save time.
- Tell them that, as they read the notes, they should underline key ideas. This will help them to identify what information and what type of word(s) they need.
- When students have finished, tell them to read through their notes to check that they make sense, that they reflect the ideas expressed in the passage and that their answers are spelled correctly. Many candidates lose marks by misspelling words when they copy them. (This includes the use of a singular form, when the word in the passage is plural, e.g. *size/sizes*.) They should also check that they have used the required number of words – students will lose a mark if they write three words

when the instructions specify no more than two.
- When students have finished the task, they can compare their answers with a partner.

Answers
6 computer science   7 program
8 adaptability   9 contact lens

8 Short-answer questions test students' ability to scan a passage for specific information or details.

As with TFNG questions, students should identify words in the questions which will help them to quickly scan the passage to find the part containing the answer. Proper names, which cannot be paraphrased, are often an obvious choice.
- Tell students that to answer these questions, they should copy words they find in the passage exactly.

2 Suggested underlining
11 problem / Energy initiative
12 'green' innovation / viruses
13 part of the university / Tim Berners-Lee
3 10 a/one quarter   11 global warming
12 electric cars   13 (the) corridors

9 Ask students to check their answers in pairs.
- Draw their attention to the bullet points in the book. To help students concentrate on producing accurate answers, you can remind them that:
  - answers must be spelled correctly, including double letters and final 'e's, otherwise they will lose the mark, although writing a American English variant instead of a British English term (and vice versa) is acceptable
  - writing one word when two gives the exact answer will lose the mark. Equally, writing three words when they are asked for two will also lose marks
  - they do need to read the question carefully. To clarify Question 10, you can ask them what the numbers 28,500 and three million refer to (the number of companies formed by MIT students and the number of employees in these companies).

10 Ask students to work in groups of four (or three if your class doesn't contain a multiple of four).
- Give each student a paper with a number (1–4) on it and tell them they are going to give a short presentation of about two minutes to answer the question with the number they have been given.
- Give them a minute or two to prepare.
- They then take turns to give their presentations to the other people in their group.

- The students who are listening should each think of a follow-up question to ask the presenter at the end of each presentation.

Speaking Part 1

❶ Ask students to look at the Exam information box.
- Point out that there is a short introduction at the start of the test, and this is not assessed.
- Explain that in Part 1, they will be asked some very straightforward questions about themselves. There are always questions on familiar topics, e.g. *travelling* or *where you live*. Suggest to students that they use Part 1 to get warmed up and start feeling confident about talking in English.
- *As a warmer* Ask students to work in pairs and think of five or six questions they think the examiner might ask them in this part. Then ask them to change partners and take turns to ask and answer their questions.
- Ask them to look at the questions in the exercise and ask: *Do any of these questions look similar to ones you asked?*
- 🎧 Play the recording for students to listen. At this level, students should be able to cope with all four speakers at once, without pausing in between.

Answers
2 pet   3 hand/yourself   4 exercise/sport

❷ 🎧 *Alternative treatment* Ask students to work in pairs and try to remember what each of the speakers said. They then listen again to check their answers.
- Point out to students that:
  - they gain marks for the range and appropriacy of their vocabulary, and that to achieve a high band score, they will have to use low-frequency vocabulary accurately
  - the answers are three to four sentences long, and that they should aim at this level to give answers of this length to Part 1 questions, as this shows their ability to link ideas, use a range of appropriate grammar and show that they can use correct pronunciation patterns.

Answers
1 hotel industry   2 full-time employment
3 very affectionate   4 high-pitched noises
5 toddler   6 really impressed   7 more aware of
8 facilities

Extension idea Ask students to work alone and think of three or four less-common words they could use to answer each of the questions so that the answers are true for them. They then work in pairs and take turns to ask and answer the questions.

❸ Tell students that they are also marked for their use of a range of appropriate grammar. Using *used to* to talk about the past is one aspect of this.

Answers
1 have   2 sit   3 think   4 seeing   5 do   6 being   7 be

Extension idea When students have finished the exercise, elicit the difference between:
- *used to do, used to doing* and *get used to doing*
- *used to do* and *would* in these contexts (see Language reference in the Student's Book (page 120) for an explanation).

If necessary, go through the Language reference with students.

❹ *Alternative treatment* Ask students to work in small groups. Tell them they are going to try to deceive other members of the group.
- First, they should work alone and complete the sentences, but three sentences should be true and three should be lies.
- They then take turns to read their sentences out to the group and the group then have to decide whether each sentence is the truth or a lie.
- Students get a point every time the group makes a wrong decision (i.e. decides the truth is a lie or a lie is the truth). The student with the most points is the winner.

Note: now is a good time to do the pronunciation work on sentence stress.

❺ *Alternative treatment 1* Give students a few minutes to work alone and think of ideas and vocabulary they can use to answer the questions before they start.
- *Alternative treatment 2* Ask students to give each other feedback on their answers. You can elicit criteria from the whole class and write them on the board, e.g.
  - *Did your partner give fairly long answers?*
  - *Were the answers well structured and coherent?*
  - *Did they use a range of higher-level vocabulary?*
  - *Did they use a range of appropriate grammar, including accurate tenses?*
  - *Were their answers always relevant?*

Extension idea Draw students' attention to the Exam advice box.
- Tell them that typical topics for Part 1 are family life, languages, traffic, shopping, weather, cooking, animals, housework and reading (you can write these on the board).
- Tell students to work in pairs and think of three or four questions which they could ask on one of the topics.
- They then change partners and, with their new partner, take turns to ask and answer questions.

Pronunciation Sentence stress 1

Ask students to look at the Speaking reference on page 100 and point out that pronunciation counts for a quarter of their IELTS score for speaking. This means that in addition to listening to their grammar, vocabulary and fluency, examiners also note how easily they can understand the candidate: candidates who speak too fast/slowly or mutter will lose marks for pronunciation; those who speak clearly and at the correct pace will do better. Explain that there are recognised features of pronunciation, and examiners want to see how well candidates can use and control these. Sentence stress is one of these features, along with things like intonation, rhythm and the pronunciation of sounds. If they stress the wrong words or too many words in a sentence, it can significantly affect the meaning and/or sound very odd; if they stress the right words, it will help their listener understand them. Students need to have a high degree of control of pronunciation features in order to achieve a high band level for this criterion.

❶ *Alternative treatment* After students have read the introduction to this section, ask them to work in pairs and predict which word will be stressed in each sentence. They then listen to check their answers.

Answers
1   *Suggested underlining*
    2 that's / (hotel) management / two   **3** cats / this / did   **4** two / toddler   **5** fitness / bit / used
2   **a**   In sentence 2, *that's* refers back to the important decision in the first sentence.
    b   In sentence 3, *this one* refers back to the cat and its difference from other cats.

❷ 🎧

Answers
1   1   don't (like) (emphasising strength of feeling) / criminals (important information) / home (important information)
    2   running (important information) / afternoon (important information) / more (for contrast) / that (referring back to *afternoon*) / energetic (important information)
    3   too (for emphasis) / anything (refers to handmade items and stresses the fact that none can be made) / hard (important information)
    4   sewing (important information) / couldn't (emphasising inability)

    5   brother (important information) / badly (important information) / he (referring to *brother*) / I do (referring to self and contrast)

Extension idea Ask students to work alone and choose one of the questions from Speaking Exercise 1. Tell them to write a two- or three-sentence answer, but not to underline any words.
*   They then work in pairs and take turns to read their answers aloud, stressing the words they feel are important.
*   Ask them to exchange their written answers and ask them to read their partner's written answer aloud. They can follow up by discussing how any changes in stress that their partner has made change the meaning or emphasis of the answer.

❸ *Extension idea* Ask students to work in pairs and look at the sentences in Exercise 2 again. Ask them to suggest another way in which each of the sentences can be stressed and read their ideas aloud to the class. The class should then say how the meaning changes.

Writing Task 1

❶ *As a warmer 1* With books closed, ask students: *How have the proportions of male and female students at university in your country or at your university changed over recent years? What reasons can you think of for those changes?* (You can treat this as a class discussion, or ask students to discuss in small groups.)
*   *As a warmer 2* Ask students to open their books, look at the Exam information box and say what the difference is between graphs, tables, charts and diagrams. (Graphs tend to be line graphs like the one shown, tables contain columns and rows of figures (see Student's Book page 37), charts may either be pie charts (see Student's Book page 38) or bar charts (see Student's Book page 37), diagrams are simple plans showing systems, machines or processes (see Student's Book page 60).)
*   Tell students that they will lose marks if they simply copy words from the task to their answer; they should rephrase the information using their own words, and this exercise shows them how to do this for the introductory sentence.

Suggested answer
The graph gives information about how many male and female students graduated from Canadian universities between 1992 and 2007.

Extension idea Ask students to look at how the information has been rephrased. Ask them if they can suggest another way of writing the introductory sentence using their own words.

❷ *Alternative treatment* Before doing this exercise, tell students to look at the Writing task instructions again and point out that they should report the main features. Ask students to work in pairs and decide what the main features are. They should then look at sentences 1–7 and say which ones they have already identified as main features.

- This exercise asks students to distinguish main features from minor (though true) details.
- Tell students that they should aim to summarise the information given to them, not provide interpretations, reasons for the information or introduce any information which is not presented in the task.

Answers
2, 4, 6, 7

❸ Tell students that in order to achieve a high band score, they will have to summarise the main features, but also support these with detailed statistical information from the graphs or chart. Ask them to look at how each of the sentences describing main features is accompanied by sentences containing supporting details.

Answers
Graduate numbers rose during the 15 years and reached their highest levels in 2007, but there were always more female than male graduates. (*paragraph 2*)
Thus the gap between the number of male and female graduates had widened. (*paragraph 2*)
A more detailed look at the graph reveals that the overall growth in numbers was not always steady. (*paragraph 3*)
Clearly, there were similar trends for male and female graduates over this period, but the number of women graduating increased at a higher rate than the number of men. (*paragraph 4*)

❹ Tell students that there is not **one** correct way to organise their answer, but dividing the graph before they start is one way of working out how to do it. This may not be applicable to all Part 1 tasks.

Suggested answer
The lines should cut the horizontal axis at 1995 and 2000. The data has been grouped according to the years.

Extension idea Ask students to compare where they have drawn lines with each other and with the suggested answer.

❺ Tell students:
- they will achieve a higher band score if their answer is clearly and logically organised. This includes writing paragraphs each with a clear focus
- it is essential to include an overview of the information at some stage in their summary, otherwise they will lose marks. This is covered in more detail in Unit 3
- their band score also depends on the choice and appropriateness of their vocabulary, with less-common words used appropriately getting them a higher mark.

Answers
1 Paragraph 2 looks at the overall rise and the gap between males and females, while paragraph 3 is a close analysis of the yearly data.
2 It is the overview.
3 **a** *less marked* **b** *more significant*
4 *widen*
5 *A more detailed look at the graph reveals …*
6 *flattened out*
7 *just over*
8 *slight*

Extension ideas
1 Ask students to copy the words and phrases focused on in this exercise into their notebooks and suggest they revise them and try to incorporate some of them in their own Part 1 answers when the time comes.
2 Ask students to read the sample answer again and highlight words and phrases they think would be useful when doing other Part 1 Writing tasks. They should also copy these into their notebooks.

❻ **Answers**
Graduate numbers rose during the 15 years and reached their **highest** levels in 2007 …
After 2000, however, graduate numbers saw their **strongest** growth rate, …

Extension idea Go through the Language reference on page 119 with students and ask them to supply extra examples for each point alongside the examples in the reference.

❼ Tell students to refer back to the Language reference when in doubt. Tell them that this area of grammar is essential for IELTS candidates to master, as they will almost certainly need it to describe any type of chart or graph.

Answers
1 steadiest   2 most popular   3 lowest   4 The most
5 greatest   6 most important area   7 one
8 favourite

Extension idea Ask students to write four or five sentences like those in the exercise to describe higher education in their country.

- When they have finished, ask them to work in small groups and compare their sentences. If they are all from the same country, do they agree that the sentences are true? If they come from different countries, they can discuss how higher education is different in each country.

Note: now would be a good time to do the Key grammar on page 17, which is on the past simple, present perfect simple and past perfect simple.

❽ Although your students have quite an advanced level of English, they may not be adept at analysing statistical data, so it is worth rounding up with the whole class after they have worked in pairs.

- Elicit that they should introduce the task by expressing the information given them in their own words. You can elicit suggestions for this, e.g. *international students – overseas students/students from other countries/from abroad; graduating – obtaining degrees*, etc.

❾ You can ask students to do the Writing task for homework. Tell them they should spend about 20 minutes writing and that they should set aside a couple of minutes at the end to check their answer.

Extension idea When students have done the Writing task, but before they hand it in, photocopy the sample answer printed below and the questions which follow and give a copy to each student.

- Ask students to
  – work in pairs and answer the questions
  – compare their answers with the sample answer and make any changes they want to their answers
  – exchange answers with a partner and comment or make suggestions for improvements to their partner's answer.
- When they are ready, they can hand their answer in to you for correction.

Answers to the questions below the sample answer
1 Paragraph 1 is an introduction, Paragraph 2 looks at the figures for 2001 across the provinces, while Paragraph 3 looks at the changes from 2001 to 2006. Paragraph 4 supplies an overview.
2 between
3 experienced
4 occurred
5 pattern

Sample answer
The chart compares the changes that took place between 2001 and 2006 in relation to the percentage of overseas students who graduated from universities in Canada.

In 2001, the proportion of students from other countries who graduated in Canada ranged from three percent in Ontario to seven percent in New Brunswick. Nova Scotia had the second highest percentage at 6.5. Five years later, the figures for most provinces had risen by two to three percent, with the exception of Alberta. There, figures fell by one percent to just over four percent.

A closer look at the chart reveals that significant growth occurred in New Brunswick, where the figures rose from seven to just under 12 percent. However, the biggest increase took place in British Columbia, where the percentage of graduates more than doubled, almost reaching almost 11 percent in 2006.

Over this five-year period, some parts of Canada experienced a considerable increase in their proportion of overseas graduates, although New Brunswick remained the province with the highest percentage overall.

Key grammar Past simple, present perfect simple and past perfect simple

❶ Tell students that IELTS candidates often make mistakes with the form or spelling of these particular verbs. When they have finished, go through the Language reference on page 115 with them.

Answers
3 fell back   4 fallen back   5 rose   6 risen
7 widened   8 widened   9 took place
10 taken place   11 experienced   12 experienced

❷ Encourage students to use the Language reference when necessary to help them answer these questions.

Answers
1 gradually fell   2 had decreased   3 have remained
4 has been   5 took place   6 have experienced
7 remained   8 had fluctuated

❸ **Answers**
2 has not always been   3 experienced   4 dropped
5 remained   6 saw   7 (had) reached   8 fell back

Unit 1 photocopiable activity
Skills for sale

Time: 60 minutes

Objectives

- To check students' knowledge of dependent prepositions
- To practise superlative forms
- To raise awareness of stress in pronunciation
- To build confidence in dealing with interview questions
- To practise vocabulary related to skills and qualifications
- To help students to get to know each other better

Before class

You will need to make one copy of the worksheet on page 16 for each student.

1 *As a warmer* Ask students: *Have you ever had to 'sell' your skills or experience during a job or university interview? Do you think it is an easy thing to do? Why? / Why not?*

2 Give each student a copy of the worksheet. Tell them that they have an important interview (for a job or a university course) coming soon, and to help them prepare, they have searched the Internet for useful videos. Tell them to look at the scripts of three video clips which they have found and to skim the video scripts to decide which candidate they think is best. Round up answers with the whole class, reminding students that there is no correct answer here.

3 Focus students on questions A–D in the scripts and tell them to choose the correct options. Check answers with the whole class.

> **Answers**
> **A** best **B** most **C** least **D** greatest

4 Tell students to complete gaps 1–9 with the correct preposition.

> **Answers**
> **1** on **2** on **3** with **4** to **5** for **6** of **7** about
> **8** in **9** in

5 Put students in pairs or groups of three. Ask them to make a list of seven questions they would ask an interview candidate and write them on the worksheet. If they find it difficult to think of questions, allow them to use some of the questions from the video scripts.

6 Tell students to look at their seven questions again and to underline the words which receive the main stress in each question. Go round and monitor as students do this. If necessary, work through some examples on the board and drill the correct sentence stress.

7 Arrange the class so that students are all working with different partners. They now take turns to interview each other using their questions. During the interviews, monitor students' use of stress and vocabulary, so that you can give feedback later on.

8 When all the interviews are finished, students return to their original partners and report back on how good their candidates were at selling their skills. Round up by asking the class to nominate the most convincing interviewee.

Extension idea If you have access to video equipment, film some of the interviews and post them on your class VLE or website.

Skills for sale

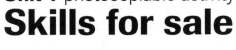

Steve: 26, Jamaican, student nurse

Alessia: 43, Italian, graphic designer

Imran: 31, Indian, IT consultant

A What do you like *better* / *best* about your current job or studies?
Well, that's a difficult question to answer, because there are a lot of things I'm keen **1** .... when it comes to nursing. In the end, though, it all comes down to the people around me, both patients and colleagues. Seeing that smile on someone's face when they get better after a period of illness, or knowing that your colleagues are relying **2** .... you to play your part in the team – that's what makes the job so special.

B Who do you admire *most* / *mostly*, and why?
I'm a big fan of Usain Bolt. He shows that it's possible to compete **3** .... your rivals, without becoming arrogant. He's an amazing athlete and he combines that with a really outgoing personality. If I can achieve even half of his dedication **4** .... what he does, I'll be proud of myself.

C What's your *less* / *least* attractive characteristic?
Well, I guess that sometimes my creative vision for the projects I'm working on can be a little too strong. Sometimes I end up feeling as if I'm responsible **5** .... everything, when actually, I could probably allow my assistants to take care **6** .... more aspects of each project. It's easier said than done, though, because I am really passionate **7** .... my work.

D What's your *greatest* / *most great* achievement so far?
I think it was my first presentation at a conference. I was presenting the results of a project I'd been involved **8** .... for over a year, so I was really nervous about how it would go. In the end, it went down really well, and getting positive feedback from members of the audience really helped me to gain greater confidence **9** .... presenting my own work.

Interview questions
1 ....
2 ....
3 ....
4 ....
5 ....
6 ....
7 ....

Word list

Unit 1

automated *adj* (13) done by machines and not people

base something on something *vp* [T] (11) If you base something on facts or ideas, you use those facts or ideas to develop it.

bring people together *vp* [T] (11) If an organisation or activity brings people together, it causes people to do something as a group.

by the time *phrase* (14) at the point when

channel resources into something *vp* [T] (12) to use energy and effort for a particular purpose

a common desire *np* [C] (11) a strong feeling of wanting to achieve or have something, felt by all the members of a group

concentrate on something *vp* [T] (12) to use most of your time and effort to do something

crucial *adj* (12) necessary to make something succeed

down-to-earth *adj* (11) practical and realistic

discipline *n* [C] (11) a particular subject of study

everyday *adj* (11) normal and used every day

extraordinary *adj* (11) very unusual, special or surprising

facilities *plural n* (10) buildings, equipment or services that are provided for a particular purpose

field *n* [C] (RS) an area of study or activity

get to the top *phrase* (RS) to succeed in getting one of the most important jobs in a particular career

go on to do something *vp* (12) to do something after first doing something else

growth rate *np* [C] (16) the speed at which something increases

high achiever *np* [C] (9) a very successful person who achieves a lot in their life

highly gifted *adj* (11) extremely intelligent, or having a natural ability to do something extremely well

human potential *np* [U] (11) people's ability to develop and achieve good things in the future

inspire *v* [T] (11) to make someone feel enthusiastic about a subject and give them the idea to do something

institute *n* [C] (11) an organisation where people do a particular kind of scientific or educational work

interact with someone/something *vp* [T] (11) If two people or things interact with each other, they speak or do things with each other.

master *v* [T] (11) to learn how to do something very well

obtain *v* [T] (17) to get something that you want

recruitment program(me) *np* [C] (RS) a series of actions intended to get people to join an organisation or work for a company

remain unchanged *vp* (17) to stay the same, not changing in any way

responsible for something *adj* (11) being the person who causes something to happen

sensors *plural n* (11) pieces of equipment that can find heat, light, etc.

take something for granted *phrase* (11) to use something all the time, without thinking how useful it is or how lucky you are to have it

telecoms *n* [U] (9) short for *telecommunications*, the process or business of sending information or messages by telephone, radio, etc.

thus *adv* (16) in this way

a vast range (of) *np* [C] (11) a very large number of different things

visible *adj* (11) able to be seen

vocational training *np* [U] (9) the learning of skills that prepare you for a job

Vocabulary extension

Unit 1

Abbreviations: *n/np* = noun/noun phrase; *v/vp* = verb/verb phrase; *adj/adjp* = adjective/adjective phrase; *adv/advp* = adverb/adverb phrase; *pv* = phrasal verb; *T/I* = transitive/intransitive; *C/U* = countable/uncountable

achieve an aim *vp* [T] to succeed in doing something that you have been trying to do

aspiration *n* [C/U] something that you hope to achieve

award a degree *vp* [T] to give someone a qualification for completing a university course successfully

conclusive results *plural n* results from a test or experiment that prove that something is definitely true

conduct an experiment *vp* [T] to do a test, especially a scientific one, in order to learn something or discover if something is true

confirm a theory *vp* [T] to prove that an idea is true

cutting-edge research *n* [U] research that is very modern and shows all the newest discoveries

dedication *n* [U] when you give a lot of time and energy to something because you believe it is very important

determination *n* [U] the desire to keep trying to do something, although it is very difficult

dissertation *n* [C] a very long piece of writing on a subject that is done as part of a university degree

doctorate *n* [C] the most advanced qualification from a university or college

extensive research *n* [U] very detailed research that involves a lot of information

fulfil a lifelong ambition *vp* [T] to succeed in doing something that you have wanted to do for most of your life

fund research *vp* [T] to provide the money for research

highlight a problem *vp* [T] to emphasise or make people notice a problem

investigate *v* [T] to try to discover all the facts about something

ongoing trials *plural n* tests happening now of something new to find out if it is safe or works correctly

painstaking investigation *n* [C/U] the process of trying to discover all the facts about something using very careful and detailed techniques

PHD *n* [C] an advanced university qualification, or a person who has this qualification

postgraduate course of study *n* [C] a course of study that someone does after getting a first degree

professional qualification *n* [C] a qualification that shows you have the skills and knowledge to do a particular job

pursue one's dream *vp* [T] to try to achieve something that you have very much wanted to do for a long time

recognise a qualification *vp* [T] to officially accept a qualification

research paper *n* [C] a piece of writing on an academic subject that contains research

scientific journal *n* [C] a magazine that contains articles about science

thesis *n* [C] a long piece of writing that you do as part of an advanced university course

thorough investigation *n* [C/U] the process of trying to discover all the facts about something using very careful and detailed techniques

undertake research *vp* [T] to do research

Unit 2 Colour my world

Unit objectives

- **Reading Section 2:** using the title and subheading; skimming; matching headings, pick from a list and summary-completion tasks
- **Vocabulary:** phrasal verbs
- **Listening Section 2:** table completion and pick from a list tasks
- **Speaking Part 2:** structuring the talk using discourse markers, managing fluent discourse
- **Pronunciation:** intonation 1 – using intonation to express positive and negative emotion
- **Writing Task 2:** analysing the task and brainstorming, planning possible answers, attitude adverbials
- **Key grammar:** nouns and articles

Starting off

❶ *As a warmer* To get students thinking about the influence and importance of colour, tell them to work in small groups and ask them to discuss these questions:
- *How do different colours affect your mood?*
- *When you are buying clothes, how important is the colour, and why?*
- *In your culture, are some colours considered luckier than others? Which ones?*
- *Alternative treatment* To encourage students to use a more extensive vocabulary, write these words on the board – *active, calm, comfortable, dynamic, excited, nervous, relaxed, self-confident, soothed, sophisticated, stimulated, upbeat* – and ask them which, if any, of the places might give them these feelings, and why.

❸ *Extension idea* Ask students to explain the reasons why the room they describe has that colour and decoration.

Reading Section 2

❶ *As a warmer* Tell students that the IELTS test often contains a reading passage on some aspect of psychology. Ask them to work in small groups and say what sort of things psychologists investigate when studying small children (*suggested answers:* relationships with parents and others, how children learn things, their language development, their ability to reason, etc.).

- Elicit the importance of reading the title and subheading (it quickly orientates you to what the passage is about and, in real life, whether or not you would be interested in reading further).

> **Suggested answers**
> Reasons why children find it hard to learn colours; some explanation of how colour words are used in English

❷ Give students a maximum of three minutes to skim the article. Be strict about the time limit. When they have finished, they can discuss the question briefly in pairs.

> **Suggested answers**
> teachers/parents, because they would like children to learn things in the best way possible;
> other psychologists, because they may be interested in researching it

A note on skimming

Even at quite advanced levels, some students have difficulties with skimming and need extensive practice – they may never have been taught to do it in their own language. Teaching skimming needs to be done in class so that you can supervise how your students read.

- Remind students that skimming involves running your eyes fairly quickly across the page, picking up groups of words as you read, but not puzzling over complex grammar or unknown vocabulary. It does not involve trying to understand the exact meaning of each sentence. It means picking up the general idea or gist of the whole passage so you have a general idea of how it develops and where you will locate answers to questions later.
- When you give a skimming task in class, give a time limit and be strict about it. Students who have not reached the end of the passage when the limit expires should stop reading anyway.
- You can supervise whether students are skimming or not by watching them as they read; students whose lips are moving, or who are reading with a finger or pen under the words are not skimming, and need to be told this. You can also watch students' eye movements as they read, to tell if they are skimming or not – if they are using the technique correctly, their eyes will be moving quickly over the text, not focusing on one place for any length of time.

❸ The aim of the matching-headings task is to test students' ability to identify the main idea or purpose of each paragraph.

Normally, when questions are printed before the passage, students should read the questions carefully before reading the passage, so they know what they are looking for when they start reading. However, here, students are asked to read each section first and note down the main theme so that they practise looking for the global idea. When they look at the headings in Exercise 4, each of their notes should match one of the headings.

- *Alternative treatment* If you wish your students to practise doing this task in the conventional way, ask them to study the list of headings in Exercise 4 first and then read the passage to do the task.

Extension idea Ask students to work in small groups and agree a heading which summarises the themes they noted down for each section (without looking at the headings list in Exercise 4).

❹ When they have matched the headings, ask students to underline sentences in the passage which gave them the answers. Remind them that there must be clear evidence in the passage to justify their choices, and that the list of headings contains distractors; the distractors will often contain words or ideas which refer to or are reflected in part of a section, but which don't summarise the whole section.

1 iv (*For some reason, however, when it comes to learning color words, the same children perform very badly.*)

2 i (*... cognitive scientists at Stanford University in California hypothesized that children's incompetence at color-word learning may be directly linked to the way these words are used in English.*)

3 iii (*To explore this idea further, the research team recruited 41 English children aged between 23 and 29 months and carried out a three-phase experiment.*)

4 vii (*As predicted, when children are exposed to color adjectives in post-nominal position, they learn them rapidly (after just five training trials per color); when they are presented with them pre-nominally, as English overwhelmingly tends to do, children show no signs of learning.*)

Extension ideas

1 If students did the extension idea in Exercise 3, ask them to discuss how the headings in the exam task are different from the headings they wrote.

2 Give students another article to read (possibly the passage in Unit 1 on pages 11–12). Ask them to work in pairs and write headings for each paragraph and

two distractors (i.e. wrong headings). They should mix their headings and distractors so they are not in the same order as the paragraphs. They then give their list of headings to another pair, who have to decide which heading refers to which paragraph.

A note about British and American English: Students may notice that the passage uses American English (e.g. *color* instead of British English *colour*), and ask which they should use in the exam. You can tell them that both are equally correct, but that they should try to use either British or American spellings consistently in their answers.

❺ Remind students to read the instructions: they often get the answer wrong by writing too many words.

- Before they do the exercise, ask students to look at the summary title and quickly find the section of the passage which will provide the answers.
- Remind students to read through their completed answer when they have finished to check it is grammatical and reflects the meaning of the passage.
- *Alternative treatment* This exercise can be done as a whole-class activity. Elicit key words around the gaps which will help students to find the correct answers (*answers*: **5** many four-year-olds still struggle **6** adjectives in a phrase or sentence **7** number of ... recognise similar objects **8** of a colour cannot be developed using the same approach **9** the way colour words ... to children).

Answers
1 Answers are in sections A and B.
3 5 training trials (*Even after hundreds of training trials, children as old as four may still end up being unable to accurately sort objects by color.*)

6 (pre-nominal) position (*In the speech that adults direct at children, color adjectives occur pre-nominally ("blue cup") around 70 percent of the time. This suggests that most of what children hear from adults will, in fact, be unhelpful in learning what color words refer to.*)

7 features/cues (*Chairs have features, such as arms and legs and backs, that are combined to some degree in a systematic way; they turn up in a range of chairs of different shapes, sizes, and ages. It could be said that children learn to narrow down the set of cues that make up a chair ...*)

8 meaning/concept ... *in this way they learn the concept associated with that word ... there is nothing systematic about color words to help cue their meaning.*)

9 unhelpful (*In the speech that adults direct at children, color adjectives occur pre-nominally ("blue cup") around 70 percent of the time. This suggests that most of what children hear from adults will, in fact, be unhelpful in learning what color words refer to.*)

❻ The aim of the 'pick from a list' task is to scan the passage to find the relevant section(s) and then read those sections in detail to answer the question.

- Remind students that, in the exam, they will not have time to read the whole passage again to find the answers. They should use words in the question to scan the passage to find the parts they need to read carefully, as they practised in Unit 1.
- Tell them they should read those parts of the text carefully and understand them before reading options A–E, as reading the options in advance may cause them to misread or misunderstand the passage.

Answers
1 *Suggested underlining*
   10–11   the experiment / true
   12-13   outcomes
2 **10–11**   Section C
   12–13   Section D
3 **10–11** (in either order)
   A (*The pre- and post-test materials comprised six objects that were novel to the children.*)
   C (*... half the children were presented with the items one by one and heard them labelled with color words used pre-nominally ("This is a red crayon"), while the other half were introduced to the same items described with a post-nominal color word ("This crayon is red").*)
   12–13 (in either order)
   C (*Only children who had been trained with post-nominal color-word presentation and then tested with post-nominal question types were significantly more accurate than chance.*)
   D (*Comparing the pre- and post-test scores across each condition revealed a significant decline in performance when children were both pre- and post-tested with questions that placed the color words pre-nominally.*)

❼ Extension idea Ask students:
- *Why do some children have difficulty learning to read or doing maths?*
- *What things cause learning difficulties in general, and what can parents and teachers do to deal with these difficulties?*
- *How are children with learning difficulties helped in your country?*

Vocabulary Phrasal verbs

Students can raise their vocabulary score by using more idiomatic vocabulary items, such as phrasal verbs.

❶ As a warmer Ask students: *What problems do you have with phrasal verbs?* If necessary, ask them to read the first sentence of the Reading passage and say which is the phrasal verb (*brought up*). Students are likely to mention the difficulty in:
- deducing their meaning from their component parts
- using them correctly
- learning/remembering them.
- Before students do the exercise, go through the Language reference on page 115 with them. Where possible, elicit further examples from them and ask them to write them down in their notebooks.
- **Alternative treatment** Ask students to find the phrasal verbs in the passage and deduce their meanings from the context before they look at the definitions (a–h).

Answers
1 g **2** c **3** h **4** e **5** a **6** d **7** b **8** f

❷ Answers
1 working out **2** pointed out **3** come up with
4 narrow; down **5** came to **6** carry out
7 turned out **8** turned up

❸ Answers
brought up (bring up): to look after a child and educate them
end up: to finally do something, especially without having planned to
come down to: If a situation comes down to something, that is the thing that will influence it most.
pick out: to choose one thing or person or several things or people from a large group
set up: to get all the necessary equipment ready for a particular activity

Extension idea (with small classes) Tell students they are going to get points for using phrasal verbs from the passage correctly themselves including phrasal verbs from Exercise 1.
- You can write the following point system on the board:
  – *Used ambitiously and correctly: 3 points*
  – *Used ambitiously, but with small problems: 2 points*
  – *Used unambitiously but correctly: 1 point*
  – *Used completely wrongly: 0 points*

- Tell students to choose four of the phrasal verbs, then create their own sentences using them. Tell them that *ambitiously* means using them in a way which tries to extend their ability with the language (including using unfamiliar phrasal verbs) and expressing themselves like someone aiming for Band 7.5 or above!
- Ask students to take turns to read their sentences to the class. Meanwhile, award points and discuss with students why each sentence scores as it does.

❹ Encourage students to refer to the Language reference on page 115 while doing this exercise.

Answers
1 bring up, work out, narrow down, carry out, pick out, set up, point out
2 come to, turn out, end up, turn up
3 come up with, come down to

Extension idea Ask students to work alone and write four sentences of their own using phrasal verbs from this section.
- When they have finished, tell them to work in small groups and take turns to read out the first half of their sentence up to the verb, but not the particles, of their sentences.
- The other students in the group have to suggest or guess how the sentence ends. (You can give them an example such as *After applying for 15 different jobs he ended ...* Students can then suggest *up on the dole, up working for Microsoft,* etc.)

Suggested answers
1 to clothes, I can never decide what to wear.
2 up with a solution to the problem.
3 up exhausted.
4 them up, as their parents were working in another city.
5 down the finalists to the top three.
6 out the importance of regular training.
7 out all these tasks.
8 out to be an incredible success.
9 up on time if you have an interview.

Listening Section 2

❶ *As a warmer* Ask students to work in small groups. Ask: *What museums are there in the area where you live, and what can people learn from visiting them?*
- Round up with the whole class by asking: *Which museum sounds the most interesting?*

Extension idea Give students a few minutes to think about an exhibition they've been to, and to prepare to talk about it for two minutes.
- When they're ready, ask them to work in pairs and take turns to give their talk.

❷ Table completion tests candidates' ability to listen for main ideas and details. It is likely to deal with facts rather than opinions.

- Before reading the task, ask students to check the rubric to see how many words they can use (one).
- Tell them to also think about what type of word they will need for each gap (a noun).
- Elicit what they should do if there is a word in the task (e.g. *camouflage*) the meaning of which they are not sure of. (*Suggested answers:* Guess the meaning from the context if that is possible; listen for the word in the context and guess; listen for an idea being expressed which may be a paraphrase of that word.) In any case, the important thing is to write a word in the gap, not worry too much about unfamiliar vocabulary around the gap.

Suggested underlining
1 gallery / huge   2 connect colour   3 learn / affects sight   4 camouflage / pick / suitable
5 room   6 music / colours / change
Suggested answers
1 something you look through
2 something to do with culture
3 something that affects the way you see things
4 something related to camouflage and animals / the natural world
5 a room connected with colour
6 something that can be coloured in a room / something that changes

❸ 🎧 Play the recording once only, but give students some time afterwards to complete and check their answers.
- Remind them that checking their answers includes making sure that they make grammatical sense and are spelled correctly.
- Tell them they should write something in every gap, even if they're not sure of the answer. In the IELTS test, marks are not subtracted for wrong answers, while an intelligent guess might just be right and gain a mark.

Answers
1 eyeball   2 lifestyle   3 disability
4 background   5 mood   6 lighting/atmosphere

Extension idea Play the recording again, for students to check their answers. They can then work in pairs to compare their answers, including the spelling.

④ ⌒ Before students do the exercise, ask them to read the Exam advice box. Tell them that the correct answers are likely to be paraphrased, while they may well hear something very close to some of the distractors.

- Tell students that underlining key words and ideas helps them to focus on the main point of the question.

> **Suggested underlining**
> 7–8   TWO colours / most popular
> 9–10 TWO reasons / children / selecting
> **Answers**
> **7** B/E   **8** E/B   **9** B/D   **10** D/B

⌒ Extension idea To reinforce the concept of paraphrasing, play the recording from Exercise 3 again and ask students to read the recording script on page 150 and underline the words which give the answers.

⑤ Encourage students to give quite long answers (e.g. two or three sentences) to each of these questions.

Speaking Part 2

❶ As a warmer 1 Write on the board: *home life, work, studying, social life, travel, shopping.* Ask students to discuss in small groups: *Imagine a world where you couldn't see things in colour, only in black and white. How do you think that would affect the way you live?* Tell them they can use the ideas on the board to help their discussion.

- **As a warmer 2** Tell students to look at the Exam information box and the task in Exercise 1. Ask them:
  1 *What do you think is being tested in Speaking Part 2?*
  2 *What is difficult about doing Speaking Part 2?*
  3 *How do you think you can get high marks doing this part?*
  (*Answers:*
  1 All the things mentioned in the Exam overview on page 7, plus the ability to speak fluently at length and to manage and structure extended discourse. Vocabulary and grammar are also assessed in the same way that they are in other parts of the test. Tell students that the purpose of the three points in the task is to help them structure their talk and give ideas to talk about. They do not need to worry about covering the points in order, or about saying an equal amount on each. In fact, they can omit a point if they have nothing to say on it. However, they must talk about the topic. If they fail to do

this, the examiner may consider their answer memorised and may not take this part of the test into account when making their assessment.)

- Ask students to look at the Speaking task. Tell them that:
  - Speaking Part 2 always has this format, with prompts the speaker should cover. Students have time to make some notes
  - although they will find this part difficult at first, they will rapidly improve with practice
  - when they do this part, they should look at the examiner and only refer to their notes and the task card to prompt them and help them keep going
  - it is important to keep going until the examiner tells them to stop. Although the instructions say 1–2 minutes, students should expect and aim to speak for the full two minutes
  - they should introduce and structure their talk, and at the end of the two minutes, when the teacher says 'thank you', start to conclude. Tell them not to worry if the examiner asks them to stop before they have finished a sentence.

- Tell students that although they are being asked to discuss the task in this exercise, in the exam itself, they do it alone with the examiner and therefore do not have the opportunity for discussion before giving their talk. Tell them the notes they make should be quite brief.

❷ ⌒ Alternative treatment If you wish, ask students to follow the recording script on page 151 while they listen.

> **Answers**
> **2** decided to buy   **3** looks pretty old
> **4** Some of my friends   **5** ultimately

Extension idea Ask students to work in pairs and suggest other ways they can introduce the points on the card. Round up with the whole class and write good suggestions on the board for students to copy into their notebooks.

❸ ⌒ Alternative treatment Before students listen, elicit why each of the strategies in this exercise is useful.

> **Suggested answers to alternative treatment**
> Avoiding hesitation shows fluency and an ability to manage language while giving time to think; phrases for when she has forgotten something allow her to omit the detail asked for in the bulleted points; clarification allows her to ensure that the examiner has understood what she means and also gives her a second opportunity to express an idea or argument; referring back allows her to go back and add in extra details to things she appeared to have finished with; paraphrasing helps her to explain when she doesn't know the word.

All these strategies help students keep going and enhance their performance in relation to the 'fluency and coherence' criterion in the bandscales.

Answers

2	let me see
3	by that I mean
4/5	as I mentioned before / as I said
6	long, thin pieces of wood

Extension idea As in Exercise 2, ask students in groups to suggest other phrases Zandra could use for each of these strategies. Again, round up with the whole class, writing good suggestions on the board for students to copy into their notebooks.

❹ Tell students that in the exam, the examiner will ask a short question at the end about the talk, e.g. *Do you still have the thing you bought?*

Note: now is a good time to do the Pronunciation section on intonation.

❺ If you think or notice that your students need help, elicit some possible colourful events, e.g. at a local festival or market, when travelling, out shopping or on holiday, etc.

- ***Alternative treatment 1*** Before students start, remind them of some marking criteria:
  - range of vocabulary – tell them to think of words and phrases which are not necessarily the easiest or simplest way of expressing things, but which describe or express things more exactly
  - range and complexity of grammar – tell them to think a little about how they can express ideas using a range of complex structures (conditionals, relative and participle clauses, etc.)
  - fluency – tell them to think about how they can link ideas together and incorporate some of the strategies they have learned in this unit to avoid hesitation and loss of coherence.
- ***Alternative treatment 2*** Tell the partner who is listening to imagine they are the examiner. They should give marks for pronunciation, vocabulary, grammar and fluency. At the end of the talk, they should:
  - ask a simple question
  - tell their partner what marks they gave them and why.

  If necessary, refer them again to the Exam overview on page 7.

Extension idea You can follow up with some Part 3-style questions like the ones below (you can write these on the board and ask students to discuss them

in pairs if you wish, or make them part of a whole-class discussion). Give students some time to think before answering the questions.

- *What things make scenes or events especially memorable for people?*
- *How do scenes and events change in people's memories?*
- *Why are people's childhood memories often so special to them?*
- *Why are the events people remember so important to them?*

Pronunciation   Intonation 1

❶ 🎧 Elicit which words are likely to be stressed in a sentence (words which carry most meaning or the speaker wants to emphasise). Tell students that most intonation – the rise or fall of our voices – happens on the stressed words.

- Remind students that using intonation well and naturally will improve their mark in the exam.
- Tell them also that marked rises and falls in intonation express enthusiasm and interest in what they are saying. This also affects the listener, in this case the examiner, who will react positively.

Answer

I mean, I've seen some terrible puppet shows in the past, but these dolls were expressive – they came alive.

Extension idea Ask students to repeat *fantastic* as Zandra says it. Then ask them to repeat *it was just fantastic*. Finally, ask them to work in pairs and read the whole sentence to each other.

❷ 🎧 Remind students to identify the stressed words first, in this case, ones which convey positive or negative emotions.

- You can do the first sentence with them. Remind students that words also have internal stress. Elicit which syllable in *fantastic* is stressed (the middle syllable).

Answers

1 I decided to buy this doll because we'd been to a puppet theatre and seen a performance, and it was just fantastic.

2 The story included a certain amount of fighting, which was probably quite frightening for children, but it was also magical – and the good guy won, which I like.

---

3 Actually, my doll looks pretty old, even though it was made – you know – made in this era.

4 It's only wooden, but dressed in really bright, attractive materials, like batik.

5 Some of my friends think she's very scary, and others, like me, are really drawn to her.

6 I feel that she protects me from bad things and brings me good luck.

❸ 🎧 *Alternative treatment* Play each sentence individually, then ask students to repeat them. When they are confident, ask them to work in pairs and read the sentences to each other.

Extension idea Ask students to work alone and write three or four sentences about something colourful they bought in the past (they could refer to the notes they made in Speaking Exercise 1). They should then decide:
– where to place the stress in the sentences
– what intonation to use on the stressed words.
When they have finished, they should read their sentences aloud to their partners and afterwards, if the class is not too large, to the whole class.

Writing Task 2

❶ *As a warmer* With books closed, ask students to work in small groups and discuss these questions (you can write them on the board):
– *To what extent do you think it is important for people to work or study in pleasant surroundings?*
– *Why do so many people have to work in unpleasant surroundings? How do you think it affects the quality of their work?*
You can round up with the whole class and turn it into a general class discussion.

• With books open, ask students to read the Exam information box. Tell them that there are sometimes two questions to discuss, or two aspects of a topic to write about. Also mention timing, and the fact that Task 2 is worth twice as many marks as Task 1. For this reason, it is important that they spend the suggested 40 minutes on preparing, writing and checking their answer to this task.

• Ask them to read the Writing task and to underline the key ideas (the things they must deal with) while they read (*suggested underlining:* how people feel / colour schemes / offices and hospitals / How true / How far does colour influence people's health and capacity for work?).

• Tell students that they must cover all parts of the task to get good marks in this part of the test; if they omit any important aspect of the task, or deal with it only briefly, they will lose marks.

• Suggest to students that they take notes while they discuss the questions in this exercise.

❷ Tell students that it is important to think and plan before they start writing. They will score higher marks for a structured, coherent essay, and they should write their answer following their plan.

• *Alternative treatment* Before they complete the plan, ask students to read the sample answer and see how many of the ideas they came up with in Exercise 1 are expressed in the answer.

Answers
2nd and 3rd paragraphs: reaction of visitors / bright colours help creativity
4th and 5th paragraphs: recovery needs calm colours / children's wards need brighter colours / staff need distraction in breaks

---

Extension ideas

1 Ask students to read the sample answer again and then, in small groups, to say if there are any ideas they do not agree with.

2 Tell students that it is essential to deal with all parts of the task. Ask them to work in pairs and check that all parts of the task in Exercise 1 have been covered adequately in the sample answer (they have).

❸ Remind students that it is important that they make their opinions clear in their essay. Attitude adverbials such as those underlined help them to do so.

• Elicit what position in the sentence attitude adverbials normally come in (*answer*: at the beginning).

• When students have finished the exercise, go through the Language reference on page 112 with them.

Answers
2 Clearly   **3** As far as I am concerned
4 The general view has been that
5 it is inevitable that   **6** Interestingly
7 As a matter of fact

Extension ideas

1 Although students may never have studied these specifically, they will know quite a few. Ask them to think of other attitude adverbials which have similar meanings to these ones.
(Suggested answers:
1 arguably – potentially
2 clearly – obviously, of course, no doubt, undoubtedly

3 as far as I'm concerned – in my opinion,
I personally believe, I think that
4 The general view has been that – Generally
speaking, Generally, In general, Most people think
that
5 It is inevitable that – It is certain that, Certainly
6 interestingly – surprisingly
7 as a matter of fact – in fact, actually, in reality)

2 • Ask students to write sentences using these
adverbials but expressing ideas from their plan in
Exercise 2.
• When they finish, ask students to read sentences
which they are not sure are correct to the
whole class, who can then, if necessary suggest
corrections or improvements.

❹ Tell students that it is important to use adverbials
such as these in their essays and that such errors are
very common.
• Where necessary, students can refer back to the
Language reference to check their corrections.

Answers
2 ~~In my opinion~~ (*What follows also introduces an
opinion, so the writer is saying the same thing
twice.*)
3 ~~In my point of view~~ **From** my point of view / In
my **opinion**
4 ~~Arguable~~ Arguably
5 ~~As the matter of fact~~ As **a** matter of fact
6 ~~As far as I concerned~~ As far as I **am** concerned

Extension idea As revision, ask students to find four
phrasal verbs in the sample answer which they saw in
the Vocabulary section earlier in this unit and to say
what they each mean (*end up* – to finally do something;
taken up – to be very busy doing something; *carry out*
– do or complete something; *come up with* – suggest
or mention). Remind them that using phrasal verbs and
other advanced vocabulary in their answers will create a
very favourable impression and improve their band score.

❺ Tell students that to do this, they can go back to the
questions in Exercise 1 to help them.

Suggested answers
2nd and 3rd paragraphs: office workers need
comfort, not colour / worry about money and
rewards / can't find a colour to suit everyone, so
doesn't matter
4th and 5th paragraphs: patients need to get better
– not worried about colour / visitors interested in
patients / staff too busy

---

❻ Point out to students that in the live exam, they
would have 40 minutes for this task. Since they have
already spent some time planning and discussing
their answer, time which in the exam would also
be spent thinking and planning, they should aim to
complete this exercise in 35 minutes. If you give this
exercise for homework, tell students to be strict with
themselves about the time limit and to avoid external
distractions while doing the task in order to give
themselves the best possible practice for the exam.

Extension idea Ask students to review the vocabulary
they have studied during this unit, including vocabulary
from the photocopiable word lists. Ask them to try to
incorporate some of what they have studied in their
answers.
• Ask students to exchange their answer with another
student's. They should read their partner's answer to
see how appropriately new vocabulary has been used
and to comment on it together.
• Students should give each other feedback and
suggestions on how to improve each other's answers
(in consultation with you where necessary).
• They should then make changes to their answers
before handing them in.

Sample answer
Colour is certainly something that influences
people. In their home lives, many of the choices
people make, with regard to consumer goods, are
based on colour. However, I would argue that in
public buildings, people have other preoccupations
and are less affected by their surrounding colour
scheme.
The colour of an office, for instance, is far less
important than a home. Offices are places where
people work, and what matters there is that
equipment or technology is functioning well, that
meetings have been organised and targets are being
met. Employees do not care about whether their
office walls are pink or green.
Obviously no one would choose to paint an office
black or such a bright colour that it distracts people
from their work. That is just common sense. If there
is a change in décor, staff might react to it initially,
but it soon becomes part of the background.
Ultimately, people are too involved in what they are
doing to be influenced by colour.
Similarly, hospital patients are unaware of the
colours around them. Instead, they are concerned
about factors such as the quality of healthcare they
receive and the qualifications and experience of
their doctors. For while a dirty hospital or poor
nursing might threaten their recovery, a pastel-
coloured ward will not.

What is more, psychologists' ideas about colour and its effect on health are not reliable. While some have argued that pastels are better because they calm people down, others suggest that lively colours are best because they make people happier. This all leads me to the conclusion that although colour has a significant role to play in our lives on a personal level, that is where its influence ends. In most public places, we are concentrating on other, more important matters and colour has little impact on us.

Key grammar Nouns and articles

❶ Answers
1 things, products, people, room, users, hospitals, patients
2 colour*, decoration, clothes, people, work, output, health
3 clothes, people
4 Thailand
* Note that *colour* can also be a countable noun, but it is uncountable in the context of this exercise.

Extension idea Ask students to suggest other examples for each category.

❷ Tell students these are only some of the rules for use and non-use of articles. When they have finished the exercise, go through the more complete rules in the Language reference on page 120 with them.

Answers
a the creative room
b the decoration of our homes, the products we buy, the clothes we wear, the health of patients
c one of the earliest things
d a room
e Thailand
f colour, people, work, output

❸ Encourage students to refer to the Language reference when doing this exercise. They can discuss their answers in pairs.

Answers
1 The 2 – 3 a 4 the 5 a 6 the 7 – 8 –

❹ Tell students that articles are a major area of error in the IELTS exam and that they should pay particular attention to this when doing the Writing tasks.

Answers
2 ~~job~~ a job 3 ~~Czech Republic~~ the Czech Republic
4 ~~the world~~ a world 5 ~~Elderly~~ The elderly
6 ~~the bright future~~ a bright future 7 *correct*
8 ~~a wrong approach~~ the wrong approach

Vocabulary and grammar review
Unit 1

Answers
1 2 of 3 with/by 4 for 5 to 6 in 7 for 8 as
2 2 has been conducted 3 had trebled
4 had already begun 5 filled
6 did not alter / didn't alter
7 have not had / haven't had 8 had just been paid
3 2 the second highest 3 the lowest
4 the most marked 5 lower 6 the greatest
7 the most stable 8 less well

Unit 2

Answers
1 2 back it up 3 came up with 4 dealt with
5 set up 6 note it down 7 put up with 8 get by
2 shade, red, colour-blind, purple, bright, pastel, turquoise, camouflage, mood, bold

E	K	O	L	M	J	D	W	H	V	I	C
S	R	I	P	U	R	P	L	E	D	M	O
H	O	D	F	A	V	S	B	P	O	I	L
A	W	E	T	O	T	R	H	O	N	F	O
D	B	R	I	G	H	T	D	I	L	P	U
E	X	S	E	F	J	B	E	G	P	D	R
A	P	A	S	T	E	L	U	R	E	B	B
Q	J	P	E	N	C	R	O	V	N	I	L
T	U	R	Q	U	O	I	S	E	T	Y	I
I	D	I	S	N	K	C	U	O	L	E	N
C	A	M	O	U	F	L	A	G	E	W	D

3 2 Apparently 3 arguably 4 Generally speaking
5 inevitably
4 2 – 3 a/– 4 a 5 the 6 the 7 an 8 the/–
9 The 10 the 11 a 12 the 13 the 14 the
15 The 16 the

Unit 2 photocopiable activity
The colour of tradition Time: 60 minutes

Objectives

- To build spoken fluency in debates
- To revise and practise attitude adverbials
- To practise structuring and developing arguments
- To revise and practise useful strategies to help fluency
- To check students' use of nouns, articles and intonation

Before class

You will need one photocopy of the worksheet on page 29 for each student.

❶ *As a warmer* Ask students what phrases or strategies they could use in the IELTS Speaking test for the following purposes:

- to avoid hesitating
- to repeat something they have already said
- if they forget a detail when describing something
- if they can't remember the exact English word for something.

Remind students that these phrases are worth learning by heart and practising in speaking tasks and presentations. You can check answers in Unit 2 of the Student's Book (page 24).

❷ Give each student a worksheet. Ask them to skim each speech bubble for the general idea. When everyone has finished reading, conduct a brief class vote to find out who agrees and disagrees with each statement. Avoid detailed discussion at this stage – there will be time for that later.

❸ Put students in pairs and get them to correct the five attitude adverbials in bold. Check answers with the whole class and remind students that these attitude adverbials are very useful when presenting both spoken and written arguments.

Answers
1. it's inevitable that
2. As a matter of fact
3. the general view has been that
4. As far as I'm concerned
5. arguably

❹ Tell students they are going to have a class debate. If you have more than ten students in the class, first split students into two or more debating groups of up to ten. You should then divide each debating group into two equal teams: 'for' and 'against'. Focus students on the debate question at the bottom of the

worksheet. Tell the teams they will discuss the points relevant to their side of the debate and add further explanations and examples of their own. Give them a few moments to prepare ideas. If they have difficulty thinking of extra examples, they can use some ideas from the speech bubbles as a starting point.

❺ The teams then take turns to speak for three minutes on each point. It is up to each team to decide who will speak on which point, and whether they will present as individuals or in pairs. Make sure that every student has an equal chance to speak at length. With less confident classes, encourage teams to rehearse their speeches as a group before they 'perform' for the class. Remind them to use attitude adverbials where relevant. After each speech, give the opposing team a chance to ask questions.

❻ Once all the points have been covered, conduct a class vote to see whether the motion has been carried or defeated. Encourage students to vote honestly based on the arguments they have heard, rather than just for their own team.

❼ After the voting, conduct a feedback session, based on any errors you may have noticed during the presentations, especially in the use of nouns, articles and intonation. Write these up on the board for students to discuss. It is also a good idea to praise examples of effective language use, to keep the feedback balanced.

Extension idea As a follow-up to the debate, set the following Writing task. Remind students of the importance of clear paragraphing and a well-balanced essay structure, framed with an introduction and conclusion (see Student's Book page 106, Writing Task 2).

Write about the following topic.

In the modern, globalised world, traditional colours associated with clothing, festivals and cultural symbols have lost their meaning. It is no longer necessary for people to pay any attention to colour in these areas.

To what extent do you agree or disagree?

Give reasons for your answer and include any relevant examples from your own knowledge or experience.

Write at least 250 words.

The colour of tradition

❝ Now that global brands are everywhere, **it's inevitably that** people's colour associations will be completely different from before. There's no way that you can ignore what you see on your TV and computer screen, day by day. **❞**

❶

❝ People's ideas for weddings are quite varied these days. **As fact matters**, some couples in my country choose to have two ceremonies: the first in traditional dress, and then another ceremony with a photographer with the bride wearing the 'international' white wedding dress. **❞**

❷

❝ Until recently, **the general viewing has been that** only dark colours are acceptable for office wear, which basically means black, grey or dark blue. Now, however, things have started to change. The other day, one of my colleagues came to work in a light green suit, which would have been unthinkable for my parents' generation. **❞**

❸

❝ Looking at our old family photos, it's clear that my parents felt that they had to dress my brother in blue, but give me pink or red clothes to wear because I'm a girl. I'm not going to do the same with my children, though. **As far I'm concerned**, there's no need to dress boys and girls in different colours. **❞**

❹

❝ Colour is **arguable that** the most important factor in global branding. Companies spend a huge amount of money and energy on making sure that their brand image is linked to a specific colour in people's minds. They envy international organisations like the Red Cross and Red Crescent which have traditional symbols that are instantly recognisable to people in different countries. **❞**

❺

DEBATE: TRADITIONAL COLOURS HAVE LOST THEIR MEANING IN THE MODERN WORLD.

For

1 importance of colour in international brands and logos

explanation:..

example: ....

2 parents' attitudes to children's clothes

explanation:..

example: ....

3 influence of the Internet

explanation:..

example: ....

Against

1 traditional clothing in local events and ceremonies

explanation:..

example: ....

2 coloured symbols traditionally used by international organisations

explanation:..

example: ....

3 conventional colour choices for clothing in the workplace

explanation:..

example: ....

Word list

Unit 2

bold *adj* (26) describes a colour which is bright and strong

camouflage *n* [U] (23) when the colour or pattern on something is similar to the area around it, making it difficult to see

colour scheme *np* [C] (25) a combination of colours that has been chosen for the walls, furniture, etc. of a particular room or building

comprise *v* [T] (20) to have as parts or members, or to be those parts or members

concept *n* [C] (19) an idea or principle of something that exists

confirm *v* [T] (20) to prove that a belief or an opinion which was previously not completely certain is true

consistent *adj* (20) always behaving or happening in a similar, especially positive, way

cue *v* [T] (20) to give someone a signal to do something

decoration *n* [U] (18) the style and colour of paint or paper on the walls of a room or building

distinguish *v* [T] (19) to recognise the differences between two people, ideas or things

draw someone to something *vp* [T] (25) to attract someone to a thing or person

entities *plural n* [C] (20) things which exist apart from other things, having their own independent existence

give someone a taste of something *phrase* (RS) to allow someone to see or experience a little of something

haphazard *adj* (19) not having an obvious order or plan

house *v* [T] (RS) to contain or provide a space for something

hypothesise *v* [I] (19) to suggest an explanation for something which has not yet been proved to be true

in an effort to *phrase* (19) trying to

in such a way that *phrase* (26) If you do something in such a way that something happens, you do it in order to make that thing happen.

in the course of *phrase* (19) during

incompetence (at) *n* [U] (19) lack of ability or skill to do something successfully or as it should be done

interactive displays *plural n* (23) collections of objects for people to look at which react when people use them and instruct them to do particular things

make predictions *vp* (19) say what will happen in the future

master *v* [T] (19) to learn how to do something well

novel *adj* (20) new and original, not like anything seen before

occupants *plural n* (26) the people who live in a building

occupy *v* [T] (26) to live in a building

one by one *advp* (20) separately, one after the other

overwhelmingly *adv* (19) very strongly or completely

parental *adj* (20) connected with parents or with being a parent

pastel colours / pastels *plural n* (26) light colours that are not strong

play a role in something *phrase* (26) to be involved in something and have an effect on it

property *n* [C] (19) a quality in a substance or material, especially one which means that it can be used in a particular way

repertoire *n* [C] all the words that you know or can produce

shade *n* [C] (18) one form of a colour, especially a darker or a lighter form

striking *adj* (RS) easily noticed and unusual

systematic *adj* (20) using a fixed and organised plan

to all intents and purposes *phrase* (RS) used when you describe the real result of a situation

to some degree *phrase* (20) partly

unique *adj* (19) being the only existing one of its type or, more generally, unusual or special in some way

Vocabulary extension

Unit 2

affect subconsciously *vp* [I] to influence in a way that we are not even aware of

alter a mood *vp* [T] to influence the way that someone feels at a particular time

background *n* [C/U] the parts at the back of a picture, view, etc. which are not the main things that you look at

cognitive *adj* (formal) relating to how people think, understand and learn

colour-blind *adj* unable to see the difference between particular colours

range of colours *np* a group of different colours

competence *n* [U] the ability to do something well

have considerable influence on *vp* [T] to affect someone or something to an important degree

contrasting *adj* If two or more things are contrasting, they are very different from each other, in a way that you notice.

convey an idea *vp* [T] to communicate an idea

developmental psychology *n* [U] the scientific study of the changes that occur in the human mind during the different stages of life

display *n* [C] a collection of objects or pictures arranged for people to look at

disproportionate amount *n* [C] an amount that is too large or too small in comparison with something else

evoke a feeling *vp* [T] to make someone feel a particular emotion

exert an influence on someone/something *vp* [T] to have an effect on someone or something

expressive *adj* showing your feelings

forthcoming *adj* willing to give information

garish *adj* unpleasantly bright in colour, or decorated too much

in layman's terms *phrase* If you explain something in layman's terms, you say it simply, in a way that someone who does not have special knowledge of a subject can understand.

language acquisition *n* [U] the process of learning a language

language proficiency *n* [U] when you can speak a language very well

negligible effect *n* [C] an effect that is so small, it cannot be noticed or considered important

pale *adj* light in colour

profound change *n* [C] a very great change

sponsor *v* [T] to provide money for an event, programme, etc. in return for advertising your own products or services

subtle *adj* not obvious or easy to notice

symposium *n* (formal) [C] an occasion at which people who have great knowledge of a subject meet in order to discuss a matter of interest

unintelligible *adj* impossible to understand

upbeat *adj* positive and expecting a situation to be good or successful

use jargon *vp* [T] to speak using words or phrases that are used or understood only by people with special knowledge of a subject

❶ Find and correct one mistake with superlative forms in each sentence. You need to either delete a word or change a word.

            most
0 The second ~~more~~ popular course at this university is medicine.

1 My most favourite subject on this course is marketing.

2 Physics is one of my less favourite subjects.

3 The most number of complaints came from students in the business school.

4 He is one of the most cleverest students in my year.

5 It is often students in their first year who do the lowest amount of study.

6 Learning to be independent is the one of the most important things I learnt at university.

❷ Complete each of the sentences below using an adverb or adverbial phrase from the box.

actually	apparently	arguably	generally speaking	~~surprisingly~~	understandably

0 The light colours they have used make the room look ....*surprisingly*.... spacious.
1 I haven't seen it yet, but .... , the colour she has chosen for her bedroom is awful!
2 .... , pink is much more popular with girls than it is with boys.
3 The Mona Lisa is .... the most famous painting of all time.
4 .... , she was very upset when her artwork was destroyed.
5 Many people think black is a dull colour, but .... , it's my favourite.

❸ Find and correct the mistakes relating to phrasal verbs in each sentence.

               come up with
0 We haven't got much time to ~~come up~~ a good idea.

1 She pointed at that they still had two more questions to answer.

2 He finally managed to narrow his options to a choice of only two.

3 It's a good argument, but you really need to back up it with more examples.

4 I'm finding it very difficult to work up a solution to this problem.

5 The points he made were important, but I didn't manage to note down them.

6 If you don't start working harder, you'll end out failing this course.

❹ **Complete these sentences by writing the correct preposition (by, for, with, to, etc.) in each gap.**

0   A vocational course prepares students ...._for_....... working life.

1   The university has an international reputation .... excellence in teaching.

2   Have you ever participated .... a research project?

3   It is more difficult to interact .... the teacher and other students in a large classroom.

4   You might find this article relevant .... your next assignment.

5   Each candidate has to compete .... hundreds of others to secure a place on this course.

6   The student welfare officer is responsible .... all non-academic issues affecting undergraduate students.

❺ **Choose the correct option in each of these sentences (– = no article).**

0   In some countries, _(the)_ / – colour red is associated with happiness.

1   White is _a_ / – colour often worn by the bride at weddings in Western cultures.

2   _The_ / – lion is one animal which suffers from colour blindness.

3   Many animals use colours as – / _the_ camouflage.

4   In China, it is common for _the_ / – young boys to wear black.

5   Colour can be important in _a_ / – country's national identity.

6   _The_ / – Netherlands' national flag is red, white and blue.

❻ **Choose the best option (A, B or C) for each of these sentences.**

0   It can take a while to ...._B_........ the different style of teaching at university.
   A be used to   **(B** get used to**)**   **C** used to

1   University fees .... much lower than they are today.
   A used to be   **B** were used to being   **C** would be

2   The first time I had to do a presentation, I was very nervous, as I wasn't used .... them.
   A doing   **B** to do   **C** to doing

3   When you were at school, ... to wear a school uniform?
   A did you used   **B** used you   **C** did you use

4   When he was a child, he .... stay with his grandparents every summer.
   A would   **B** used   **C** was used to

5   She .... enjoy the subject at school, but she loves it now she's at university.
   A wouldn't   **B** didn't use to   **C** didn't used to

❼ **Complete this paragraph by writing the correct form of the verb in brackets in each gap.**

Overall, the number of applicants to Central University (0) ....._has increased_..... (increase) in recent years, but since 2006, the different faculties (1) .... (show) slightly different trends. Between 2008 and the present day, there (2) .... (be) only a very small rise in applicants for Engineering compared to the previous two years, when a significant increase (3) .... (take place). Up until 2009, applicants to the Business School (4) .... (fall) slightly each year for three years, but after this date, numbers (5) .... (rise) steadily each year until 2011 when they (6) .... (reach) a peak before decreasing slightly over the next year.

Unit 3 A healthy life

Unit objectives

- **Listening Section 3:** matching, flow-chart completion, listening for paraphrased meaning
- **Reading Section 3:** using the title, subheading and illustration; skimming; summary completion with a box, Yes / No / Not Given, multiple choice
- **Vocabulary:** verb + noun collocations
- **Speaking Part 2:** talking about plans, ambitions and aspirations connected with health
- **Pronunciation:** linking and pausing
- **Writing Task 1:** analysing and linking two sources of information; planning; paraphrasing words from the task; identifying key features; writing an overview
- **Key grammar:** expressing large and small differences

Starting off

❶ *As a warmer* With books closed, tell students that this unit's topic is health.
- Ask them to work in small groups and, between them, think of five ways to stay healthy.
- When they have finished, round up ideas with the whole class.

> **Answers**
> 1 d 2 b 3 f 4 c 5 a 6 e

Extension ideas

1 Write *cure* and *treat* on the board. Ask: *Which means to make someone with an illness healthy again?* (*answer:* cure). *Which means to give medical care?* (*answer:* treat)
2 To teach some verb–noun collocations connected with health, write these words and phrases on the board: *pain, disease, injury, broken bone, operation.*
   - Ask students to look at the captions and decide which verbs they can use with each of these nouns – more than one answer may be possible (*suggested answers:* treat, relieve, cure, reduce pain; catch a, cure disease; treat, sustain an injury; treat, set a broken bone; undergo an operation).

❷ **Answers**
   1 v 2 iii 3 i 4 iv 5 ii 6 vi

❸ *Extension idea* Ask: *Which of these things are free and which do you have to pay for in your country? Which do you think should be free?*

Listening Section 3

❶ *As a warmer* To further activate the vocabulary seen in Starting off, ask students to work in small groups and give them two minutes to think of names of different types of health worker, e.g. *physiotherapist.* (*Some possible answers:* doctor, nurse, radiologist, surgeon, general practitioner, consultant, psychiatrist, first-aider, pharmacist/chemist, optician, ambulance driver)
- Ask: *What do each of these people do?*

> **Suggested answers**
> 1 Providing therapy, treatment and exercises to help people regain full movement in limbs, etc. You can point out that the first part of the word *physio* refers to the body, while a *therapist* is someone who makes people feel better / grow stronger. It can be used in other medical areas, e.g. *speech therapist.* The adjective *therapeutic* is used to describe something that causes someone to feel happier and more relaxed or to be more healthy, etc.
> 2 after you have received treatment for an illness or injury related to your bones, joints, etc.

❷ Matching tasks test ability to listen for information and details, opinions, attitudes, purpose or the general gist.

Students do not have time before listening to analyse or process the questions in depth, but since they hear the recording only once, they need to focus as clearly as possible before they listen. Tell them that underlining key ideas in the questions helps them to do so. Moreover, they should not worry if they feel they need to underline the whole phrase or sentence, especially when these are very short.

Suggested underlining

A strengthens / whole body
B most popular
C special sportswear
D most effective
E evening
F rarely

Extension idea Remind students that the comments will almost certainly be expressed using other words when they listen to the recording. Ask them to work in pairs and suggest other ways to express each of the comments.
(*Suggested answers:* **A** It makes all of the body stronger. **B** This is the one which most people ask for. **C** We employ a small apparatus. **D** This works better than any other. **E** It is most effective if you do it late in the day. **F** We don't often use this.)

❸ 🎧 Give students some time to check their answers.

Extension idea If you wish, play the recording again for students to check their answers, but remind them that they won't have this opportunity in the exam.

Answers
1 D   2 A   3 F   4 B   5 E

❹ Flow charts test students' ability to understand a series of linked events, or a process.

Ask students: *What should you expect to hear when the listening task involves completing a flow chart?* (*answer:* people describing stages in a process)
• Remind students that they should:
  – read the rubric to check how many words they can write
  – look at the title, so that they know what the conversation will be about.

Suggested answers
1 an example of what happens during a visit to the clinic
2 6 a type of injury (beginning with a vowel)
  7 related to ankle injury   8 aspect of treatment (beginning with a vowel)   9 aspect of a joint
  10 type of person

Extension idea Ask students in pairs to decide the type of word(s) they need for each gap. (**6** noun beginning with vowel   **7** noun   **8** noun beginning with vowel   **9** noun   **10** noun beginning with consonant sound).

❺ 🎧 *Extension idea* If you wish, play the recording again for students to check their answers.

Answers
6 (existing) injury   7 (the) damage   8 exercise plan   9 movement   10 personal trainer

❻ Point out to students that they will rarely hear the same words in the recording as in the questions – these will be paraphrased, so they are always listening for something which carries the same meaning but is expressed differently.
• Remind students that if they cannot remember the exact words, they should write down words that express the same idea. Sometimes a slight variation on the exact words may be accepted as correct.

Answers
1 1 it gets results more quickly than anything else
  2 it works on everything and gives you more power / we improve your overall form
  3 I guess you don't use it much? / we tend to avoid it most of the time
  4 It's what everyone asks for / it outstrips all our other services
  5 people come at the end of the day for this
2 6 turn up   7 assess   8 design
  9 monitor   10 oversee

Extension idea If students did the Extension idea in Exercise 2, ask them to compare the answers here with the answers they gave in Exercise 2.

❼ Give students a minute or so to think and make some notes before they speak.

Extension idea You can round up by asking two or three students to speak about the topic for a minute or two to the whole class.

Reading Section 3

❶ *As a warmer* Ask students: *When you visit the doctor, which is more important: how the doctor talks to you, or the treatment you are given? Why? Do you think doctors can sometimes cure patients just by being sympathetic? Why?*

❷ Point out that any illustrations which accompany a Reading passage in the exam are intended to help students understand the subject, and should be looked at carefully.
• Students should discuss their answers in pairs or small groups.

Suggested answer
An improvement in someone's health resulting from the administration of a fake (not real) drug; a change in attitudes towards the placebo effect among the medical community

❸ Give students two minutes to skim the article and be strict about the time limit.
• When they have finished, ask them to discuss their ideas in pairs, but without looking back at the article.

4 Yes / No / Not Given (YNNG) questions test students' ability to scan for specific information and then to read the relevant part of the passage in detail to fully understand the writer's ideas or opinions.

Tell students that:

- these questions are similar to True / False / Not Given (TFNG), but whereas TFNG questions deal with facts and information, YNNG questions deal with a writer's opinions and claims. Explain what a claim is (*answer:* something that the writer believes to be true, but that cannot be proved and that other people might not believe). Students do not need to worry too much about this distinction, but should expect to see the words *claims* or *opinions* in the rubric. (When you come to Question 5, you can point out that although the key contains Potter's claims, the writer also agrees with them by saying *As Potter says*)
- as in TFNG questions, unless the question specifically contradicts an idea or opinion in the passage (a 'No' answer), the answer is 'Not Given'
- some of the words or phrases in the question will be the same as or similar to words in the passage. Students should scan the passage to find similar words and then read carefully around to decide their answer.

Suggested underlining

1 Merck's experience / MK-869 / unique
2 unsuccessful test results / well-established drugs company
3 medical conditions / easily treated / placebo
4 third group / Kaptchuk's trial / better
5 Kaptchuk's research / combined drug and placebo treatments / avoided

Answers

1 NO (*MK-869 has not been the only much-awaited medical breakthrough to be undone in recent years by the placebo effect.*)
2 YES (*In today's economy, the fate of a well-established company can hang on the outcome of a handful of tests.*)
3 NOT GIVEN (*Medical conditions are mentioned, but there is nothing about their relative response to a placebo.*)
4 YES (*Not surprisingly, the health of those in the third group improved most.*)
5 NO (*Studies like this open the door to hybrid treatment strategies that exploit the placebo effect to make real drugs safer and more effective. As Potter says, "To really do the best for your patients, you want the best placebo response plus the best drug response."*)

---

5 Summary completion tests understanding of ideas expressed in the passage. Students will need to skim and scan to find the relevant parts of the passage.

Point out to students that:

- having skimmed the passage already, they should be able to find the paragraphs quickly
- when underlining the key ideas in the summary, they should focus on the information and type of words they need to complete the gaps.

Answers

1 the first two paragraphs (They contain references to Merck and MK-869.)
The third paragraph mentions MK-869, but goes on to discuss other issues.
2 *Suggested underlining*
 6 concerns / increasing   **7** Merck / increase / anti-depressant market   **8** Initially / MK-869
 9 key / treated   **10** indicated / pointless

---

6 **Answers**

6 H (*... Merck, a global pharmaceutical company, was falling behind its rivals in sales. To make matters worse, patents on five blockbuster drugs were about to expire, which would allow cheaper generic products to flood the market.*)
7 A (*Key to his strategy was expanding the company's reach into the anti-depressant market ...*)
8 C (*The drug tested extremely well early on ...*)
9 G (*True, many test subjects treated with the medication felt their hopelessness and anxiety lift.*)
10 E (*Ultimately, Merck's venture into the anti-depressant market failed. In the jargon of the industry, the trials crossed the "futility boundary".*)

---

7 Multiple-choice questions test students' ability to skim or scan to find the relevant section of the passage and then to read in detail and discriminate between the correct answer and distracting information.

Students should use the stem of the multiple-choice question (e.g. in Question 11 *Which of the following is true of William Potter's research?*) to help them find the part of the text which answers the questions before looking at options A–D. Students are often confused by looking at the options first and then reading the text to find the correct answer. In most cases, better results are obtained by understanding the text first and then finding the option which corresponds.

Vocabulary Verb + noun collocations

❶ *As a warmer* Write *feelings* on the board, and below *express*, *provoke*, *prepare* and *promote*.

- Tell students that one of the verbs does not collocate with feelings. Which one? (*answer:* prepare)
- Ask them what each of the collocations means (answers: express feelings – say how you feel; provoke feelings – make someone/people feel in a certain way; promote feelings – encourage particular feelings)
- Tell students that they will achieve a higher band score if they can use advanced collocations effectively when they speak or write.

Answers

1 c 2 f 3 e 4 g 5 h 6 b 7 a 8 d

❷ **Answers**

1 devised 2 determine 3 overlooked 4 promote
5 gauging 6 challenged 7 outline 8 yielding

Extension idea Ask students to work in small groups and discuss the following.

1 a therapeutic treatment that they feel is often overlooked

2 a popular viewpoint that they would like to challenge

3 how they would determine the salary of a doctor or nurse

4 how easy or difficult they find it to gauge how good a doctor is

5 the importance of exercise in promoting a sense of well-being

- As a whole-class round-up activity, ask the groups to take turns to 'challenge' other groups to explain their views on one of the five points, e.g. 'Natasha's group – tell us about a popular viewpoint that you would like to challenge.'
- Students from the 'challenged' group should then answer with what they discussed.
- You can allow this to develop into a class discussion if you wish.

Speaking Part 2

❶ *As a warmer* Write the following on the board: *diet, stress, travel, work, where you live*. Ask students to work in small groups and discuss how these things can affect people's health.

- *Alternative treatment* Ask students to work alone. Give them a minute to make notes on the task, as if it were an exam situation. When they have finished, ask them to work in pairs and take turns to give their talks. **Note:** if you do this alternative treatment, you should also do the alternative treatment for Exercise 5.

❷ 🎧 Tell students that in the exam, they are given a separate piece of paper for making notes – they cannot make them during the task itself.

Answers

what ... like to do	a triathlon
what ... involve	swimming, cycling and running events; no breaks
when ... do it	when the academic year is over; in a year's time
why ... good for my health	healthy; get fitter; eat well; plenty of sleep

Extension idea Ask students to compare the completed notes with the ideas they discussed in Exercise 1. Ask them:

- *What things do you think it is useful to put in your notes: ideas or vocabulary, or both?*
- *How much should you write? Or is it better just to think through what you're going to say and think of ways to express it?*

- **Note:** there are no correct answers to these questions, which depend on each individual student.

❸ 🎧 Ask students what all the sentences have in common (*answer:* They talk about the future, Faris's hopes and ambitions).
- Go through the Language reference on page 120 with students.

> **Answers**
> **1** taking part   **2** could   **3** to finish
> **4** to tackle   **5** doing   **6** 'll be

❹ Tell students to complete the sentences with fairly long answers, e.g. *When I have taken my IELTS test, I expect to complete my medical training at Guy's Hospital in London and then return to my country as a qualified surgeon.*

> **Answers**
> 1 When I have taken my IELTS test, I expect to (be) …
> 2 I have always dreamed of (being) …
> 3 I hope one day I (will/can be) …
> 4 This year, I am looking forward to (being) …
> 5 If I have a holiday next year, I am likely to (be) …
> 6 I have always wished I (could be …), but I might find (being …) too difficult.

❺ *Alternative treatment* Do this alternative treatment if you did the alternative treatment in Exercise 1.
- Ask students to do the task in Exercise 1 again with the same partner. When they have finished, ask them to discuss:
  - *How was your answer different this time?*
  - *Did you use any of the language you have just studied?*
  - *Did it improve your answer?*
  Note: now is a good time to do the Pronunciation section on linking and pausing.

❻ Tell students to try to incorporate phrases and structures from Exercise 3 in their answers.

Pronunciation Linking and pausing

❶ *As a warmer* Ask students: *When you read something aloud in English, do you pronounce all the letters?* (*answer:* no) *Are English words always pronounced the same way, or does it depend, for example, on the stress or their position in the sentence?* (*answer:* the stress and position in the sentence)

- 🎧 You may need to play the recording several times, but elicit the rule in the answers below.

> **Answers**
> **1** not pronounced   **2** pronounced
> Because the *t* in extract 2 is followed by a vowel; in extract 1, it is followed by a consonant.

❷ 🎧 Tell students to use the rule they deduced in Exercise 1 to decide the answers here.

> **Answers**
> 1 *triathlon's a:* /z/ pronounced
>   *sport event:* /t/ pronounced
>   *rather a:* /r/ pronounced
> 2 *for when:* /r/ silent
>   *I'd take:* /d/ silent
>   *part in:* /t/ pronounced
>   *not sure:* /t/ silent
> 3 *I'm actually:* /m/ pronounced
>   *forward to:* /d/ silent

❸ Round up by asking selected students to read sentences out to the whole class, who should listen and say how correctly they have read them.

❹ 🎧 Students should find most of the links given in the Answer key below by following the rule of 'consonant + vowel'. However, you may need to explain to them that a final *d* is often dropped if the next word begins with *t* (e.g. *need time*) and a final *t* is often dropped if the next word begins with *p* (e.g. *get plenty*).

> **Answer**
> That would be realistic because I'd need time to train and really get into shape. It's not something that I could do in a hurry! Um, obviously it would be a really healthy thing to do because it would force me to get even fitter than I am now. Plus I'd have to eat well during the training period and get plenty of sleep and that sort of thing.

Extension idea Ask students to write three or four sentences which they might use to answer the task in the Speaking section Exercise 2.
- When they have written them, they should mark how they link words.
- Ask them to work in pairs and take turns reading what they have written and linking the words correctly.
- To follow up, give them time to think about how they would answer the whole Speaking task, using what they have learned about linking words. Then ask them to take turns to do the task.

Writing Task 1

❶ *As a warmer* Write on the board:
- *People are living longer.*
- *People are having children later.*
- *People are having fewer children.*

Tell students to work in small groups and ask: *Which of these phenomena are happening in your country? What are the reasons for this? How will this affect your country in the future?*

- When students look at the chart and table, point out that they have quite a lot of detail, but a limited number of general trends, which the details fit clearly.
- Tell students that they will sometimes have to describe and summarise information from two or three different types of source, and it is important to see how the information is related.

Answers
1 Both are about population figures in Japan, but the table refers to one sector of the population – the over–65s.
2 Key features are:
   a the rise in the general population to its peak in 2005;
   b the increase in the ageing population and the ageing population as a proportion of the whole population;
   c the predicted overall fall in the population. General trends can be identified across the data and often form part of the overview, while key features are specific key points that stand out within the data.
3 The proportion of elderly people is increasing; overall population figures have risen and are predicted to fall.

Extension idea Ask students: *If you were asked to produce a similar chart and table for your country, what key features and general trends would it show?*

❷ Ask students to compare their plans with another pair before reading the sample answer.

❸ Point out to students that there are several possible ways of organising the information and that this sample is just one of them.

Suggested answer
Paragraph 1 (Introduction): Topic and time period
Paragraph 2: Population figures 1950–2005
   A comparison with the percentage of over–65s during this period
Paragraph 3: Population figures 2005–2055
   A comparison with the percentage of over–65s during this period
Paragraph 4 (Overview): A reference to two contrasting trends and a smaller, older population

❹ For Question 1, tell students that they must quote some figures from the charts to support their description, otherwise they will not achieve higher than a Band 5 for this task.

- Remind them that the instructions tell them to make comparisons where relevant, so that they should look for similarities and differences to describe.
- They will achieve a higher band score for a well-organised, coherent answer, and using linkers effectively helps to achieve this.
- It is essential to include an overview of the information. Answers which do not include one will not achieve more than a Band 5 for this task.

Answers
1 figures at key points in the data: the start (1950); the mid-point (2005) and the end of the timescale (2055)
2 to highlight the key features / main trends that the writer goes on to summarise
3 the rise in both the general and ageing population up to 2005 (a parallel increase); *while*
4 the fall in the general population against the rise in the ageing population (two contrasting trends); *However, In spite of*
5 to provide a one- or two-sentence summary of the overall trend(s) in the data

❺ Remind students that:
- they will achieve a higher band score by using advanced vocabulary accurately
- it is important that they use their own words in their answers. They will lose marks for lifting directly from the wording of the task.
- Ask them to copy the words and phrases from this exercise into their notebooks. Tell them to review it before doing other writing tasks in this course.

Answers

1 a over 65 / above the age of 65 / older people / the ageing population / elderly people
   b Japan's general population figures / number of people / overall population / total population figures / the number of people living in Japan / Japanese people / Japan's demographics / citizens
2 a (just) over b considerably; substantially
   c parallel d a little below e at a faster rate
   f contrasting g greater numbers of

Extension idea Ask students to suggest other words/ phrases with similar meanings where possible; you can also use the suggestions which follow (*suggested answers:* more than – slightly more than / (slightly) in excess of / exceeded; similar – corresponding; a little below – somewhat less than, just short of; at a faster rate – at a faster pace; contrasting – distinct/diverging; greater numbers – larger numbers).

• When they have finished, ask students to:
  – write their own examples using these words/ phrases, or
  – say how they could be used to replace the phrases in the sample answer, or
  – rewrite the sample answer using some of these words and phrases.

❻ Suggested answers

1 Key features are:
   a the higher consumption of fatty food in Group B;
   b the higher consumption of fruit and vegetables in Group A;
   c the negative effects on health and well-being of Group B.
2 the different quantities of the various types of food eaten by the two groups; the weights and relative levels of illness and attendance for the two groups
3 a reference to the link between what is eaten and health
4 either describe each chart in turn or compare the charts then describe the table

Extension ideas

1 Ask students to work in pairs and write a plan for the answer to this task.
2 Ask students *Which pie chart would most closely reflect diets in your country?*

❼ Answers

1 Key features: However, the amount of high-fat food eaten by Group B is considerably higher than in Group A, at 50 percent, while students in Group B eat far fewer vegetables than Group A and a slightly smaller quantity of fresh fruit. The table indicates that there are twice as many overweight people in Group B (20 percent) as in Group A. What is more, Group B has experienced a much higher level of illness over the year, with over double the number of students being absent from classes.
2 Paragraphs 2 and 3 consist of comparisons.
3 The second sentence is the overview. (The first sentence is the introduction.)
4 The writer compares the charts, then discusses the table.

Extension idea Ask students to write a brief plan for this sample answer. If they did Extension idea 1 in Exercise 6, ask them to compare the two plans.

❽ Answers

1 types 2 aspects 3 levels
4 amount/quantity/proportion
5 amount/quantity/proportion
6 amount/quantity/proportion
7 level/incidence/rate 8 number 9 rate

❾ Answers

1 rate 2 quantity 3 proportion
4 aspect 5 incidence 6 level

❿ Answers

1 amount 2 aspects 3 proportion
4 number 5 levels 6 rate

Note: now is a good time to do the work on comparisons in the Key grammar on page 39.

⓫ *Alternative treatment* If you feel your students need in-class preparation for this task, you can ask them the following questions and elicit the suggested answers in brackets:

– *How are the charts related?* (The table gives information on health spending and life expectancy for some of the countries in the chart. The chart covers an aspect of health spending.)
– *What are the key features?* (the ratio of beds to 1,000 people in Japan / the high level of spending in the US against the lower levels of government support / the link between Japan's government spending and life expectancy)
– *What similarities and differences are there, and how would you highlight them?* (similarities: spending figures for Netherlands and Canada;

low number of hospital beds for six of the countries and higher numbers for three countries. differences: Japan's allocation of hospital beds vs. health spending in the US (high and low))

- *What should your overview include?* (wide differences in spending; no obvious correlation between levels of health spending and number of hospital beds; little impact on life expectancy)

Sample answer

The chart and table reveal some significant differences between the countries, with regard to health and medical care.

Looking at the chart, it can be seen that Japan provides by far the highest number of hospital beds, at 14 per thousand of the population. The second highest allocation is 8 per thousand in Germany, but this is little more than half the Japanese figure. On the other hand, the US, Spain, Canada and the UK provide the lowest numbers of hospital beds, at around 3 per thousand people. Dutch and Australian figures are only very slightly higher than this.

The table takes a closer look at funding and life expectancy in three of these countries. Although Japan has a much better life expectancy figure (83 years) than the other two countries, its government spends considerably less money on healthcare, contributing just $2,581 per person. In contrast, the US government allocates well over twice that amount, yet its citizens have a life expectancy of only 78 years. Meanwhile, Dutch people can expect to live to be 80, and the government spends $3,481 on each citizen.

Although the Japanese government contributes much less money to healthcare, there are far more beds available for patients, and people can expect to live longer there than in some other countries.

Key grammar Expressing large and small differences

❶ Tell students that Writing Task 1 always asks students to make comparisons, so this area of grammar is essential.

- When students have finished the exercise, go through the Language reference on page 113 with them.

Answers
1 very
2 *less* and *fewer*; fewer is used with countable nouns
3 considerably; much
4 far (a big difference); slightly (a small difference)
5 over double the number / twice as many … as

❷ Elicit why *smaller quantity* replaces *less* in the example (they mean the same).

Answers
2 Some people's sleep patterns are very/totally/ entirely/quite different from/to mine.
3 There are far / considerably / a lot fewer injuries among pedestrians now.
4 Alternative medical treatment is becoming much / a lot / far more popular in my country.
5 Now that I'm seeing a physiotherapist, I have much / far / a lot less pain.
6 Inoculations have resulted in a lower incidence of childhood illness.

Extension idea Ask students to look back at the charts and tables in the Writing section and write five of their own sentences comparing data in the charts. Tell them to refer to the Language reference when necessary, and to try to use constructions they find difficult.

❸ **Answers**
1 very   2 lower   3 many   4 smaller and smaller
5 as

Unit 3 photocopiable activity
RLV-692 on trial

Time: 40 minutes

Objectives

- To revise and practise collocations connected with health and medical treatment
- To practise making comparisons
- To practise describing data from two sources of information
- To practise using phrases that express amount, quality, category and extent
- To raise awareness of linking and pausing when speaking
- To build spoken fluency in a discussion format

Before class

Make one photocopy of the worksheet on page 43 for each student.

❶ As a warmer Ask students how easy they think it is for a drug company to produce a new product. Can a new drug be prescribed to patients as soon as it has been produced in the laboratory? Elicit the idea of clinical trials, and tell students they are going to be responsible for investigating a new painkiller called RLV-692.

❷ Put students in pairs. Give each student a copy of the worksheet and get them to complete the summary with the words in the box. Check answers with the class.

> **Answers**
> 1 alleviate   2 clinical   3 determined   4 leader
> 5 treated   6 response

❸ Put students in groups of three. Ask each group to decide who will play each role: the marketing manager of the drug company which has developed RLV-692; a doctor who is concerned about patient safety; and a chairperson. Each student reads about their role on the worksheet. (If there is a group of four or five, the latter roles can be covered by a pair of students.)

❹ Once everyone is ready, the marketing manager and the doctor take turns to speak for two minutes each, using data from the charts to back up their arguments. The chairperson's role is to time each talk and then conduct a discussion for a further five minutes, based on the questions that have been prepared. During the discussion, monitor unobtrusively, noting down any errors in the use of comparatives or phrases that express amount, quality, category and extent. You may also wish to assess students' pronunciation of consonant sounds when words are linked.

❺ After the discussions have finished, the chairperson conducts a vote to see whether RLV-692 should receive permission to be sold on the market, or whether it should be subject to further clinical trials. To ensure that there is a clear outcome, the chairperson may vote.

❻ After voting, each chairperson reports back to the class with their result and a summary of the discussion. Other people in the group can comment on the chairperson's summary.

❼ Conduct a feedback session, based on any errors you may have noticed during the discussion phase. Write these up on the board for students to discuss. Be sure to point out examples of both correct and incorrect language, without mentioning which student made the errors.

Extension idea Students write an objective description of the two charts on the worksheet in at least 150 words, paying particular attention to language of comparison. Remind students that in Writing Task 1, they should only describe the information given, not interpret it. Give them a maximum of 20 minutes to write their descriptions, before asking them to check each other's work.

Unit 3 photocopiable activity
RLV-692 on trial

Summary

alleviate	clinical	determine
leader	response	treated

A new drug, codenamed RLV-692, has been developed by researchers, who believe it may be effective in helping to
1 .... pain. However, RLV-692 must undergo a series of **2** .... trials before it can be prescribed for use by the general public. The drug company which plans to market RLV-692 needs to provide scientific proof that the new product is both effective and safe, and doctors need to be convinced that their patients will benefit from using the drug without risks of any significant side effects. The success of RLV-692 will be
3 .... by the results of these trials. The charts below give information about the results obtained in one recent trial which compared RLV-692 with Product A, a widely available drug which is currently the market
4 .... The charts give data about the effects on different groups of subjects
5 .... with each drug. In this trial, patient
6 .... to the drug was assessed on the basis of the number of hours of pain relief after taking a standard dose.

Speaker 1
You are the **marketing director of the drug company** which has developed RLV-692.
You want to convince the rest of the group that RLV-692 is a safe and effective drug which should be allowed to enter the market. You feel that it compares favourably with the current market-leading drug, Product A.
You have two minutes to put forward your case, with detailed reference to the graphs below, before the discussion begins.

Speaker 2
You are a **doctor** who regularly prescribes different drugs, including Product A, to patients of different ages. Your main concern is patient well-being, and you believe that new drugs should only the enter market when both effectiveness and patient safety are guaranteed.
You have two minutes to put forward your case, with detailed reference to the graphs below, before the discussion begins.

Speaker 3
You are **responsible for chairing the discussion**.
You should give each of the others two minutes to put their case, before opening the discussion for a further five minutes.
Before the discussion begins, should prepare some detailed questions to ask the other speakers, using data from the graphs below.

Chart 1

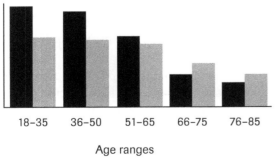

Average number of hours of pain relief after taking a standard dose

Key
RLV-692
Product A

Age ranges: 18–35, 36–50, 51–65, 66–75, 76–85

Chart 2

	side effect	patients in trial (%)
Product A	none recorded	98
	vomiting	1
	dizziness and vomiting	1
RLV-692	none recorded	95
	vomiting	0
	dizziness and vomiting	5

omplete IELTS Bands 6.5–7.5 by Guy Brook-Hart and Vanessa Jakeman with David Jay © Cambridge University Press 2013

Word list

Unit 3

absenteeism *n* [U] (38) when someone is frequently not at work or at school

behind the scenes *phrase* (33) If something happens behind the scenes, it happens secretly, or where the public cannot see.

breakdown *n* [C] (38) a way of presenting information in which things are separated into different groups

clinical trial *np* [C] (33) a test of a new medicine in which people are given the medicine

comb through something *vp* [T] (33) to search something very carefully

condition *n* [C] (33) an illness

conversely *adv* (33) used to introduce something that is different from something you have just said

cure *v* [T] (30) to make someone with an illness healthy again

demographics *n* [U] (37) the quantity and characteristics of the people who live in a particular area, for example their age, how much money they have, etc.

empathy *n* [U] (33) the ability to imagine and understand how someone else feels in their situation

evaluate *v* [T] (31) to consider something carefully and decide how good or important it is

fall behind (someone) *vp* [I/T] (32) to make less progress than other people who are doing the same thing

high stakes *plural n* (33) great advantages that could be gained in a situation and great disadvantages that could also be the result

hinge on something *vp* [T] (33) to depend completely on something

inoculate *v* [T] (30) to give a weak form of a disease to a person or an animal, usually by injection, as a protection against that disease

joint *n* [C] (30) a place in your body where two bones meet

to make matters worse *phrase* (32) used before you describe something bad that happened, making a bad situation even worse

medication *n* [C/U] (33) medicine that is used to treat an illness

open the door to something *phrase* (33) If one thing opens the door to another thing, it makes it possible for that second thing to happen.

parallel *adj* (37) happening in a similar way

pharmaceutical *adj* (32) relating to the production of medicines

plaster cast *np* [C] (30) a hard covering that is put over a broken bone in order to support and protect it while it heals

(good/bad) posture *n* [U] (RS) If someone has good posture, their back and shoulders are straight when they stand and sit; if someone has bad posture, their back and shoulders are curved and not straight.

prescribe *v* [T] (33) to say what medical treatment someone needs

receive physiotherapy *vp* [T] (30) to get treatment for an injury which involves doing special exercises and movements

rehabilitation *n* [U] (RS) when someone who has been ill or injured is cured and can do what they used to do before their illness or injury

relieve *v* [T] (30) to make pain or a bad feeling less severe

sedentary activities *plural n* (RS) activities which involve sitting and not being physically active

sleep patterns *plural n* (39) Someone's sleep patterns are their sleeping habits, for example, how much they usually sleep and when they usually sleep.

sports injury *np* [C] (30) damage to your body caused by doing a sport

substantially *adv* (37) by a large amount

symptoms *plural n* (33) physical feelings or problems which show that you have a particular illness

therapeutic *adj* (33) helping to cure a disease or improve your health

therapy *n* [C/U] (31) a type of treatment for an illness or injury

treat *v* [T] (30) to give medical care to someone for an illness or injury

undergo *v* [T] (34) to experience something, for example, a medical treatment

a wave of something *np* [C] (33) a period in which there is an increase in a particular type of activity

well-being *n* [U] (33) A feeling or sense of well-being is a feeling of being healthy, happy and comfortable.

 Complete IELTS Bands 6.5–7.5 by Guy Brook-Hart and Vanessa Jakeman with David Jay © Cambridge University Press 2013 `PHOTOCOPIABLE`

Vocabulary extension

Unit 3

administer treatment *vp* [T] (formal) to give medicine or medical help to someone

ailment *n* [C] an illness

chronic illness *np* [C/U] an illness that continues for a long time

complementary medicine *np* [U] ways of curing and preventing illness which are not used by most doctors and which are used instead of or in addition to conventional medicine, for example homeopathy

complexity *n* [U] when something involves a lot of different but connected parts, in a way that is difficult to understand

contract a disease *vp* [T] (formal) to get a serious disease

debilitating illness *np* [C/U] (formal) an illness that makes you physically or mentally weak and unable to do things

deteriorating health *np* [U] when the condition of your body is becoming worse

diagnose *v* [T] to say what is wrong with someone who is ill

disorder *n* [C] a disease or mental problem

diversity *n* [U] when many different types of things or people are included in something

exposure to infection *phrase* the state of being in a situation in which you may get an illness from another person

frequency *n* [C/U] the number of times something happens in a particular period, or the fact that something happens a large number of times

health scare *np* [C] a situation that causes a lot of people to suddenly worry that a particular thing might make them ill

incapacitate *v* [T] (formal) to make someone too ill or weak to work or do things normally

incurable disease *np* [C] a disease that is impossible to cure

jeopardise health *vp* [T] to do things that might harm the condition of someone's body

mainstream medicine *np* [U] ways of curing and preventing illness that are used by most doctors and which are generally considered normal

onset *singular n* The onset of something is the start of something, usually something unpleasant, such as illness.

outbreak *n* [C] when something unpleasant and difficult to control starts, especially a disease or war

practise medicine *vp* [T] to work as a medical doctor

preventative treatment *np* [C/U] something which is done to try to prevent an illness from starting before that illness develops

severe headache *np* [C] a very bad pain in the head

wellness *n* [U] health and happiness

withhold treatment *vp* [T] to not give someone medical treatment

Unit 4 Art and the artist

Unit objectives

- **Reading Section 1:** using the title and subheading to predict passage structure; skimming; table completion; flow-chart completion; True / False / Not Given
- **Vocabulary:** collocations and expressions with *make, take, do* and *have*
- **Listening Section 4:** note completion; understanding the structure of a listening text; deciding on the type of information needed
- **Speaking Parts 2 and 3:** preparing and giving two Part 2 talks; introduction to Part 3; generalising and distancing
- **Pronunciation:** speech rate and chunking
- **Writing Task 2:** analysing the task; brainstorming; arguments for and against a point of view; writing introductory and second paragraphs; expressing one's opinion clearly; introducing one's own and other people's arguments; writing conclusions
- **Key grammar:** expressing purpose, cause and effect

Starting off

❶ *As a warmer* With books closed, ask students to work in small groups. Tell them that everyone, in one way or another, is creative – for example, they can cook or dance or sing. Ask students to work in pairs and tell each other in what ways they are creative.

Answers
1 1 c 2 a 3 b 4 e 5 d
2 *Suggested answers*
   1 in an art gallery   2 in a museum / on a person
   3 in an outdoor public place, e.g. a park
   4 in an urban area
   5 in a museum or private collection

Extension idea Ask students to work alone and put the works of art in order, from most beautiful to least beautiful.
- When students are ready, ask them to work in small groups and explain the order they decided and the reasons for their decisions.

❷ *Extension idea* Ask students to work in pairs or small groups and discuss these questions:
- *What 'art works' do you have in your home?*
- *How important is art in your life?*

- *Which art forms interest you most or do you most enjoy? Why?*
- *What can you learn from looking at works of art?*
- *Why is it important to be surrounded by beautiful things?*

Reading Section 1

❶ *As a warmer* Refer students to the poster in Starting off. Ask students:
- *What was its purpose, and how successful do you think it was?*
- *How are the purposes of posters different from the purposes of other art forms?* (*Answer:* They are usually either for publicity advertising businesses or entertainment, or for political propaganda, as well as being decorative or for self-expression.)
- For the second question, ask students to point out features of the poster in Starting off. If students have problems answering this question, elicit the ideas contained in the suggested answer.

Suggested answers
1 in shop windows / on walls / at stations / in shops
2 pictures, bold colours, large print, black and white letters, eye-catching designs, etc.

❷ **Answer**
chronologically – showing the stages in poster design

Extension idea Ask students to express, in their own words, what they expect to read about in the article (*answer:* how the design of posters has evolved from their invention until the present day).

❸ Elicit how Reading Section 1 in the exam is different to Reading Sections 2 and 3 (*Answer:* It is generally descriptive and factual, while Sections 2 and 3 may contain argument and/or opinion; it is often slightly shorter.)
- Elicit (to remind students) why they should skim the passage in the exam (*Answer:* To get an idea of its structure and contents, so that when they come to the questions, they can scan to locate the answers more quickly).

- Tell students that they should skim this passage in just two minutes. Be strict about the time limit.
- *Alternative treatment* After you have elicited how Reading Section 1 is different, ask: *What should you do in the exam before skimming the passage?* (*Suggested answers:* Check the time on your watch and when you need to finish the section; quickly glance at the tasks to see what question types you will have to deal with.)

> **Answers**
> metal type, wooden type, router, pantograph, lithography, three-stone lithographic process, photo offset, photography, International Typographic Style, computer graphics

❹ This task tests students' ability to scan for information, using words already in the table to help them locate answers.
- Point out to students that in the live exam, they would do a combination of the three parts of Exercise 4 simultaneously, i.e. they should check what information they need for Question 1, decide where they need to look in the passage for the answer to Question 1 and answer it. Then do the same for Question 2.
- Remind students that they should:
  - always check the rubric to see how many words they can use in their answers, as this varies
  - also check the title and the row and column titles, as these will help them to locate the correct section(s) of the passage more quickly
  - copy words from the passage exactly to fill the gaps. The words need to fit grammatically and be spelled exactly the same as in the passage.
- *Alternative treatment* Ask students to do the three parts of Exercise 4 simultaneously as suggested in the note above.

> **Answers**
> 1 *Suggested answers*
>   1 another problem area   2 something related to the method itself   3 something that wood type lacked   4 something you write with / a tool for designing posters   5 something that reflects an image
> 2 The title suggests that the answers are at the start of the passage; the categories on the left side of the table connect with the first four paragraphs.
> 3 1 storage (space)   2 invention   3 colour/color and design / design and colour/color   4 (greasy) crayon   5 transfer paper

Extension ideas
1 When they have finished, ask students to compare their answers in pairs.
2 Remind students that although alternative American and British spellings will always be accepted for answers to questions (e.g. *color/colour*), to be safe, they should copy the words exactly as they are spelled in the passage. They will lose marks for misspelled words.

❺ Ask students if they made any of these mistakes themselves. Ask what other mistakes they made, and discuss why.

> **Answers**
> 1 This is ungrammatical – an adjective or noun is needed.
> 2 This is the name of the invention – it doesn't go with *another*, i.e. wood type was one invention and the pantograph was another invention.
> 3 *Both* prompts two answers, but only one is given here (the British spelling is acceptable).
> 4 *Greasy* is misspelled.
> 5 *Paper* alone is not enough, as this is a special type of paper.

Extension idea To reinforce the points made by this exercise, go through the Exam advice with students when they have finished.

❻ Flow-chart completion tests students' ability to scan to locate specific information using words on the chart to help them.

Tell students that the flow chart will always have a title, and this will help them locate the part of the passage they need to concentrate on.
- Ask: *Which question appears to need a three-word answer? Why?* (Answer: Question 6, because it is preceded by *both*)

> **Answers**
> 1 *Suggested answers*
>   6 two things which were used together or placed together on coloured posters
>   7 something posters were used for
>   8 something connected with posters by Cheret in particular
>   9 something posters represent
> 2 6 words and images   7 mass communication   8 exhibition   9 (unique) cultural institutions

❼ Remind students that in TFNG tasks:
- there will always be words in the questions which are the same as or similar to words in the passage, allowing students to scan to find the relevant parts of the passage
- they may sometimes have to scan parts of the passage where they have already answered questions, as different tasks may cover parts of the passage which overlap.
- Scanning is a speed-reading activity, so give students two minutes to identify the key words and locate where the information is in the passage. Be strict about the time limit.
- When students have finished answering the questions, ask them to compare their answers in pairs. Where they disagree, they should refer back to the passage to justify their answers.

Answers
1 *Suggested underlining*
   10 1950s / photographs / illustrations
   11 Typographic Style / modern-day
   12 Typographic Style / global
   13 Weingart / Basel
2 **10** False (*By this time, … the use of photography in posters, begun in Russia in the twenties, started to become as common as illustration.*)
   11 True (*It became the predominant style in the world in the 1970s and continues to exert its influence today.*)
   12 True (*It was perfectly suited to the increasingly international post-war marketplace, where there was a strong demand for clarity.*)
   13 Not Given (*Weingart is mentioned, but nothing is said about where his ideas originated.*)

---

❽ *Extension idea* Ask:
- *What was the original purpose of your favourite posters?*
- *Which do you prefer: modern posters or posters from the past? Why?*

Vocabulary Collocations and phrases with *make, take, do* and *have*

❶ Ask students to pay particular attention to the prepositions used with these phrases and to copy them into their notebooks.

Answers
2 had   3 took   4 made   5 taken   6 made

Extension idea Check students know what the phrases mean by asking (and possibly writing on the board for students to copy into their notebooks):
Which means …
- *considered or remembered when judging a situation?* (taken into account)
- *improve or develop something?* (make advances in)
- *influenced something?* (had an impact on)
- *made the greatest effort possible?* (did their best)
- *used something that was available?* (made use of)
- *used the good things in a situation?* (took advantage of)
(definitions based on the *CALD*)

❷ *Alternative treatment* Ask students to do this exercise, using their dictionaries to help them. At the same time, they should check the meanings of any phrases they are not sure about.

Answers

make	use (of)
	advances (in)
	a prediction (about/regarding)
	someone aware (of)
	a profit (from)
	mistakes (with)
	a decision (about/regarding)
	a choice (between)
	someone better
	an impression (on)
take	advantage (of)
	(into) account
	an interest (in)
	action (on)
	(into) consideration
do	your/their best
	business (with)
	better
	research (on)
	damage (to)
have	an impact (on)
	an interest (in)
	an influence (on)
	an effect (on)
	advantages (for)
	a result (on)
	benefits (for)

---

❸ Suggested answers

2 make a prediction   3 has many / several / a number of advantages   4 did / have done some / a lot of / considerable damage   5 have (had) an influence   6 make a decision / make a choice   7 took an interest

Extension idea Ask students to write their own sentences for five other phrases in the box. They can then read them out to the whole class, or hand them in to you to check.

Listening Section 4

❶ *As a warmer* Ask students to work in small groups. Ask:

- *What are the traditional art forms in your culture?*
- *How important are they nowadays, and how much do people value them?*
- *To what extent is art an important part of your cultural identity?*
- When students have finished, you can round up the discussion with the whole class.
- Refer students to the Exam information box and ask them to highlight or underline the following information: *one speaker, formal talk, academic topic, no break, note-completion.*

Extension idea When students have answered the three questions in the exercise, ask them if there is any similar art in their country.

❷ Note-completion tasks test candidates' ability to follow the main ideas and structure of a talk and to extract specific information and details.

Point out to students that quickly looking at how the notes are structured on the page and what information they need for each gap will help them follow the talk more easily and focus on what they should listen for. Tell them they should also pay attention to the title, as this will help orientate them to the subject of the talk.

- Ask students which gaps might need a plural noun as the answer or part of the answer (*answers:* 1, 2, 3, 5, 6, 8, 9 and 10).
- Remind students that, in the live exam, they have time at the end to transfer their answers to the answer sheet, so as they listen, they should note down their answers (or possible answers). At the end, they will have time to make sure they spell the words correctly, that the words match the information they need, and are grammatically suitable.
- Remind students to check the rubric to see how many words they can use. Tell them that the rubric in this activity allows them to use a number, in addition to a maximum of two words.

Answers

1   First section on ancient art – includes sections on cave art and ochre, which must have been a type of paint
Second section on modern art

2   1   an art form
    2   something that affects preservation of art
    3   an example of something made in dot paintings
    4   a purpose or function
    5   a substance
    6   a length of time
    7   a form
    8   a substance
    9   a substance or a tool
   10   objects that can be decorated

❸ 🎧 Tell students that they should answer with actual words they hear. If they don't quite catch the actual words, but feel they have understood the meaning, they should use words which convey the meaning (an example of this is Question 4, where *storytelling* is the word they will hear, but *telling stories* would be an acceptable answer, conveying exactly the same information and showing understanding).

- When you check the answer to Question 6, ask if it would be possible to answer the question using only words, i.e. eighteen thousand years (*answer:* No, because that would be three words – the rubric says two words and/or a number). Tell students that even when they can write the number as words, it is always correct, and usually safer, to write it in figures because that way they will avoid spelling mistakes.
- Students may ask how they will know when to write one word or two – in some cases, e.g. Question 10, one word or two are acceptable. Tell them that there are no hard-and-fast rules for this. If they have clearly heard two words which would complete the meaning satisfactorily, they should write both. If, as in Question 1, one word alone would not satisfactorily complete the gap, they should complete it with two. In the case of Questions 8 and 10, if they have clearly heard both words, it is safer to write them both, spelled correctly.

Answers

1 Body/body art   2 (the) weather   3 animal tracks   4 story(-)telling / telling stories   5 iron oxide   6 18000/18,000/18 000 years   7 powder   8 bush honey   9 canvas   10 (musical) instruments

❹ Tell students to give quite long answers – two or three sentences if possible – to each of these questions, and that *I don't know,* or *I'm not sure* are not sufficient answers, even if this is not students' area of expertise.

Speaking Parts 2 and 3

1 *As a warmer* Ask students to work in pairs and to tell each other what their favourite piece of art is, and why. Tell them it could be a film, a book, a photo or a piece of music. It needn't be a picture or a sculpture, but can be if they wish.

- Tell students that they are going to work on Speaking Parts 2 and 3 together because the Part 3 questions are always on the same topic as the Part 2 talk, and Part 2 leads into Part 3.
- Tell them that, as in this case, the task sometimes contains examples to help them.
- Remind them that in Part 2, they will have one minute in the exam to think and make notes before they speak, so it is important to choose something they can talk about confidently for two minutes.
- Although the instructions say one to two minutes, they should aim to speak for two, until the examiner asks them to stop.

2 • Ask students in pairs to add other words and phrases to the table that they think might be useful.
- Round up by asking for suggestions from the whole class, which you can write on the board.
- *Alternative treatment* Elicit and write the following checklist on the board:
  Did your partner …
  – *introduce their talk?*
  – *deal with all the points in the task?*
  – *structure the talk clearly?*
  – *use a range of vocabulary?*
  – *speak for no less than two minutes?*
- Ask students who are listening to use the checklist to give feedback to their partners when they have finished speaking.

Extension idea If you feel they need more practice at this stage, ask students to think of a second object and take a minute to prepare. They can then change partners and give another talk.
- Ask the student who is listening to give feedback using the checklist in the alternative treatment above.

3 Go through the Exam information box with students. Tell them that, as in Part 1, they answer questions. However, unlike Part 1 where the questions are personal, here the questions are about their opinions and ideas on abstract topics, and they are expected to give general answers rather than talk about themselves.
- Tell them that the examiner will have sets of questions of increasing levels of difficulty, and with high-level students who are performing well, the examiner will select a more challenging set of

questions that enables the candidate to perform to the best of their ability.
- Remind students that they should answer the questions at length.

4 **Answers**
1 The first answer (Lee's) is personal, whereas the second answer (Majut's) is general.
2 The general one (Majut's)

5 Elicit the meaning of *on the whole* (*answer:* generally).

Answers
1 most children   2 seem to

Extension idea Elicit other phrases which could be added to the table in each column (*suggested answers:* generalising about people/places, etc.: generally, generally speaking, in general; the majority of people, some people, a lot of people, etc.; verbs to generalise: appear to, tend to).

6 Give students a moment to think how they can answer the questions in general before they speak.

Extension idea You can round up answers with the whole class and turn the questions into a general class discussion if students are interested.

7 🎧 Go through the Language reference on page 114 with students. You can also refer them to the Speaking reference on page 97.

Answers

introducing a general point	generalising about people /places, etc.	verbs to generalise
on the whole broadly speaking generally	most (children) the majority of (pre-school children) older (students) a lot of (head teachers) many (educational institutions)	seem (to) tend (to)

8 Tell students that a lot of errors which candidates make at this level tend to be due to carelessness. It is important, when speaking, to correct yourself when you notice you have made a mistake, and doing so will cause a positive impression on the examiner, who will notice that you are monitoring and taking care with the way you speak.
- For item 3, elicit what *as a whole* means (*answer:* as a group, altogether) and elicit why it would not be correct (*answer:* because it conflicts with *a lot*).

Note: Now is a good time to do the pronunciation work on chunking with students.

9 Tell students that this exercise is not an opportunity for discussion: one student should ask the questions and the other should answer each of them at some length (then they swap roles).

- *Alternative treatment* Students should take turns to assume the role of the examiner. After they have listened to their partner's answers, they should give feedback on the following points (which you can write on the board):
  Did your partner:
  - *answer at length?*
  - *give general, considered answers?*
  - *answer the question exactly and relevantly?*
  - *pause naturally when speaking?**
  * Students will need to have worked through the Pronunciation section to assess this properly.

Pronunciation   Speech rate and chunking

1 *As a warmer* With books closed, ask students:
- *Why do people pause when speaking?* (to breathe, to choose a word/think what to say next, for dramatic effect, to check their listeners' reactions)
- *Are some places in sentences more natural than others for pauses? Which ones?* (We tend to pause before chunks of meaning, very often to choose the next combination of words we are going to use, before and after conjunctions and other linking phrases, where in written language we would use commas or full stops.)
- Refer students to the introductory paragraph for this section and discuss it as necessary with them. Play the recording to illustrate the point it is making.

Answer
Speaker 3 is the easiest to understand because she speaks at a regular pace and pauses between meaningful chunks of language.
Speaker 1 is harder to understand. Although the speed is OK, she pauses too frequently and the pauses do not occur between meaningful chunks of language.
Speaker 2 is also hard to understand because he speaks very fast and fails to pause often enough.

Extension idea Ask students to look at the recording script for Speaker 2 on page 154.
- Play the recording again and ask students to mark where he/she pauses.
- You may have to play the recording several times.
- Draw students' attention to how the pronunciation chunks also form groups or chunks of meaning.
- Ask students to work in pairs and take turns to read Speaker 2's answer to each other.

2 Tell students that chunking and pausing do not follow fixed rules, but very much depend on the individual speaker and the circumstances, and that there may be a variety of natural ways to chunk and pause.
- As a comment on the question, point out that speaking fluently and naturally does not require the speaker to speak as fast as possible, but to speak at a pace which he and his listeners find comfortable, e.g. you are likely to speak more quickly to your friends, who are used to your voice and speaking style, than you would in a formal situation to a stranger, such as occurs in a speaking exam.
- Point out to students that the commas have been removed from Naresh's answer to avoid giving clues to the pauses.

Answers
Well, I think broadly speaking / they can learn a great deal. / The majority of pre-school children, for example, / are incredibly creative / and experiment with paints and all sorts of other art materials, / and they just love getting their hands dirty. / Older students tend to be less enthusiastic, / but many of them still enjoy art / and, / well, / I guess if you don't try it, / you won't know whether you're any good at it.
It is well paced – not too fast or too slow.

Extension idea Ask students to work in pairs and take turns to read Naresh's answer to each other.
- If you think it's suitable, ask one or two students afterwards to read Naresh's answer to the whole class.

3 Make sure that students understand that the commas have been removed from Naresh's answer, as in Exercise 2. Play the recording several times, as necessary. Remind students that the answer on the next page reflects Naresh's chunking, but is not the only way to chunk this answer.

Answer
Well, generally, / there are quite a few reasons. / These days, / a lot of head teachers seem to be more concerned about exam results / than giving the students an all-round education. / That's obviously going to have an influence / on how significant art is in the school curriculum. / Another possible reason / is that many educational institutions / don't tend to have the money / to provide all the materials you need for art courses. / They seem to be more worried about buying technological equipment these days.

❹ *Extension idea* When students have finished, ask them to close their books and take turns to express Naresh's ideas using their own words, but pausing where it is natural to do so.

❺ Tell students to write quite a long answer (several sentences) to this question.

Writing Task 2

❶ *As a warmer* With books closed and students in small groups, ask them to tell each other about their experiences of studying arts-based subjects at school (drawing, crafts, music, theatre, etc.). Ask: *How useful do you think these subjects were?*

- With books open, remind students that it is essential to analyse the task before they start writing: they must answer it exactly. If they miss essential points from the content, they will be marked down; similarly, if their answers contain material which is irrelevant to the task, they will also lose marks.

Alternative treatment Ask students why the following would not be answering the task exactly:
- only writing about art (the question is about arts-based subjects)
- writing about primary-school children (the question refers to the secondary-school curriculum)
- not writing about overall academic performance (this would omit part of the question).

- Tell students that if they do not answer the question exactly, or omit essential parts of the question, their score for their answer may fall as low as Band 4 or 5, hence the need to underline and check that they are including all elements in the question in their answer.

Suggested underlining
arts-based subjects / compulsory / secondary-school curriculum / improve / academic performance

❷ *Alternative treatment* Divide the class into an equal number of small groups.
- Tell half the groups that they should brainstorm arguments **for** the topic and the other half that they should brainstorm arguments **against** the topic. Tell them all they should try to brainstorm more than three arguments.
- When they are ready, ask students to form new groups with a balance of **for** and **against**.
- They then discuss the topic, offering their ideas for and against and complete the diagram with the ideas they think are most useful.

Suggested answers
2 broadens general knowledge
3 improves self-discipline
4 takes up too much time
5 seen only as fun
6 money needs to be spent on resources

❸ **Answers**
1 Mika: I agree (with the former statement); I believe (that)
Tom: Obviously; it's true that; However
Dhillon: I tend to feel (that)
2 a Mika's   b Dhillon's   c Tom's

Alternative treatment Ask students to read the three introductory paragraphs, but **not** to answer the questions yet.
- Tell students that first impressions are very important in real life and when writing answers to exam tasks. Tell them to work in pairs. Ask them:
  - *Which paragraph do you most agree with? Why?*
  - *Which paragraph do you think is the best introduction? Why?* (Note: All the paragraphs are good openers, so this question is a matter of taste or opinion.)

Extension idea Ask students to note the phrases which answer the first question in their notebooks, then think of other phrases which introduce opinions and note these down as well.
- Give them any of these suggested answers which they haven't suggested themselves: *My feeling is that ..., From my point of view ..., I hold the view that ..., I firmly/strongly believe that ...*

❹ Even at this level, there are candidates who do not write their answers in paragraphs: they either write one long paragraph, or they start a new paragraph with each sentence, or they don't divide their paragraphs logically. IELTS candidates who fail to write in clear paragraphs will lose marks for lack of coherence and organisation. Tell students that:
- each paragraph should deal with a clearly different aspect of the topic

– it is helpful to have a sentence in the paragraph which states the main idea of the paragraph. Other sentences may contain supporting points, reasons, examples and effects or consequences. When students move on to a new idea or a different aspect of the topic, they need to start a new paragraph

– every sentence within a paragraph should be logical and clearly related to sentences that come before and after it

– overlong paragraphs become difficult to read and follow and, in an essay of 250 words, should be avoided. Between four and six paragraphs in an essay of this length is good number to aim for, although more might be possible, as long as each has a distinct main idea and students have the time and competence to write them.

Answers
1 Mika: It is generally thought that activities in the arts can help students learn how to work in a team. / I would suggest that experiences like these can enhance a student's ability to work with different types of people and participate successfully in a group project.
Tom: Art, it seems, can have a positive influence on students, but it could also undermine their sense of well-being.
2 Mika: second, third and fourth sentences; she uses examples (a theatrical production and an orchestra).
Tom: first, second and third sentences; he uses reasons (exercising the imagination / a break from work and schoolwork and stress).
3 Mika presents a main advantage of studying art; Tom presents an advantage and a disadvantage.

Note: now is a good time to do the Key grammar on expressing purpose, cause and effect.

5 Tell students that when you write an academic essay, it is important to show you are aware of other people's ideas and opinions, and it is useful to introduce other people's views, even if later you are going to show why you disagree with them.
• Remind students that a large part of academic work in any area consists of examining and commenting on other people's opinions and conclusions.

Answers
Mika: It is generally thought (that), I would suggest (that)
Tom: People ... claim that, they say, others would argue that

Extension ideas
1 Ask students to suggest other phrases that can be used to introduce other people's opinions. Write suitable ones on the board and ask students to copy them into their notebooks.
• They can then check their ideas with the ways of introducing arguments mentioned in the Language reference on page 114.
2 Ask students to work alone and write three opinions that other people hold (on any subject they like) and to write a follow-up sentence for each, where they state their own position on the same subject, all using phrases for introducing opinions.
• Students then work in small groups and read out what they have written.
• Where they wish, students can discuss the opinions which have been expressed.

6 Elicit from students what impression the errors in this exercise will give the examiner (clearly a negative impression, as they tend to be the result of carelessness). Tell students that these mistakes are frequent at their level and that careful writing and checking will improve their band score.

Answers
1 ~~agree~~ agree with   2 ~~claimed~~ claim / have claimed   3 ~~I'm tend to agree~~ I (tend to) agree
4 ~~believe~~ believed

7 **Suggested answers**
2 Teachers generally believe that ...
3 I tend to disagree with the view that ...
4 I would agree with the statement that ...
5 Critics claim that ...

8 When students have finished, ask them to compare their answers with a partner.

Answer
c, e, a, d, b
Suggested answer
Another way in which I feel the arts can help students is that they can improve self-confidence. This is because art is often about making a product. It might be something concrete like a painting or object, or it might be something abstract like a piece of music. Both types of product need plenty of time and creativity and, as a result, can make someone feel very proud of the outcome. I believe that this sense of achievement may then stimulate someone to achieve more in other subjects.

Extension idea Ask students to focus on linking devices within the paragraph. Ask them:

- *Which sentence states the main idea of the paragraph, and what phrase links the paragraph to the paragraph which came before?* (c) Another way in which the arts can help students is …)
- *Which sentence provides an explanation for a statement? How is it linked to the statement it explains?* (e) This is because …)
- *Which sentence supplies an example, and how is this linked to the explanation?* (a) It might be something concrete like …)
- *Which sentence explains a consequence, and how is this linked to the examples?* (d) Both types of product …)
- *Which sentence introduces a further consequence, and how is this linked to the previous consequence?* (b) This sense of achievement … (linked to very proud)).
- Students should then see how the whole paragraph has been constructed, and you could make this explicit by writing on the board:
  main idea – explanation of idea – example – consequence – further consequence

❾ Tell students that to write the conclusion, they will need to read through Mika's paragraphs again and make sure what her point of view is.

- Elicit what the conclusion should contain (*suggested answer:* a summarising point of view and a summarising explanation from that point of view, reformulating ideas already expressed in the essay, not introducing new ideas).
- Suggest that one or two sentences are probably enough.
- **Alternative treatment** Before writing the paragraph, in order to sensitise students to the need to plan and to write a balanced answer to the question, tell them to read the paragraphs from Tom's and Mika's answers to the task in Exercises 3, 4 and 8 and complete a diagram for Tom and Mika's points of view, similar to the diagram in Exercise 2.

> **Sample answer**
> In my view, all students would benefit from the creative experience that art can offer. Improved confidence and inter-personal skills are lasting qualities that can help students do better throughout their academic lives.

❿ *Alternative treatment* If you wish, students can do the preparatory work for this writing task in class in pairs or small groups, following steps they practised earlier in this section, i.e.

- underline the key ideas in the task (*They should underline:* modern painters / sculptors / huge sums of money / others / struggle / government / resolve / unfair situation / agree or disagree)
- brainstorm ideas
- formulate a position
- write a brief plan/diagram including examples. Their diagrams could be similar to the diagram in Exercise 2.
- Before they do the task, ask them to check for words and phrases in the various sample paragraphs and in the Language reference which they could use in their own answer.
- They should write their answer alone.

> **Sample answer**
> Artists, like many creative people, have to work hard to survive on the income they receive from selling their products. Some artists become popular and can charge a lot of money for their work, while many others never achieve success. I think there are good reasons why this happens, and there is nothing that governments can or should do about it.
> Generally, people are willing to pay for something that they admire and would like to own. In the case of art, this may be because they feel something is unique, or is exceptionally beautiful or skilful. Whatever the reason, I would argue that it would be quite unfair for any government to prevent the artist from asking a high price for it. Surely the public has to decide what something is worth, even if it means that less admired artists find it hard to earn a living?
> In many respects, artists are like business people. Those who can sell a lot of their work develop a reputation and can raise their prices over time. This may seem unfair to others who remain unknown, but if they choose to continue with a career in art, it seems they must accept the situation. In most cases, popular artists have spent years developing their skills, studying their subject and exhibiting their work. Why should a government deny them the earnings they have worked so hard to achieve?
> Ultimately, people have to be free to spend their money as they wish. If this means that some artists have to make the difficult choice of finding another way to earn a living, no one can alter that fact. After all, not much in life is fair!

Key grammar
Expressing purpose, cause and effect

❶ ❷ Tell students that in order to achieve a high band score in IELTS, they will have to write complex, but clear sentences, and one way to do this is to combine the purpose, cause or effect into the same sentence as the main idea.

- Elicit from students that *otherwise* introduces an effect that does **not** occur: in Tom's paragraph in Writing section, Exercise 4, students will get stressed if they feel they <u>do not</u> have time to do their schoolwork.

Answers

purpose	cause	effect
with the aim of for in order to so that	due to because of	otherwise as a result

Extension ideas

1 Ask students to suggest other words/phrases for each category.
2 • Ask students to choose four of the phrases from Exercises 1 and 2 and write sentences using them.
   • When they have finished, ask them to work in small groups and compare their sentences.
   • round up by asking students to read out sentences their group is not sure about to discuss and correct if necessary.

Suggested answers

purpose	cause	effect
with the intention of so as to with the objective of for the purpose of to + *infinitive*	owing to because due/owing to the fact that	as a consequence in consequence consequently with the effect that with the result that

❸ *Alternative treatment* If you wish, you can go through the Language reference with students **before** they do this exercise, so that they can then refer to it.

Answers
1 As a result   2 so that   3 in order to
4 because of / due to   5 for   6 otherwise

Extension idea Ask students to complete sentences 1–6 starting with the same words but using a different phrase from this Key grammar section and completing the sentence to express a different purpose, cause or effect, e.g. *The artist was awarded a government grant in order to enable him to work on his project full time.*

❹ Answers
1 because   2 because of   3 so that   4 for
5 On the other hand   6 so that

Vocabulary and grammar review
Unit 3

Answers
1 2 determines   3 promote   4 gauge   5 overlooked
  6 devised   7 outline
2 2 rates   3 types   4 quantities   5 level   6 number
  7 incidence
3 2 dream   3 likely   4 hope   5 expecting   6 I'd like
4 2 nearly   3 marginal   4 considerably/far; as

Unit 4

Answers
1 2 make   3 makes   4 has been done   5 have had
  6 took   7 made   8 had taken / had had
2 2 the   3 large   4 as   5 cases/situations   6 on
3 1 It can be argued that artists have a considerable impact on everyday life.
  2 Artists are sometimes thought to be less talented than they used to be.
  3 The wealthy have a tendency to purchase art for investment purposes.
  4 Personally, I tend to agree with the view that graffiti is the most interesting modern art form.
  5 Pablo Picasso is often said to be one of the most influential figures in 20th-century art.
  6 Children, it seems, are better / Children seem to be better able to express themselves through art than adults.
  7 The majority of historians claim that art has played a key role in cultural development.
4 2 with the result that   3 owing to   4 otherwise
  5 so that   6 has resulted in   7 with the intention of

Unit 4 photocopiable activity
Keep your distance! Time: 50 minutes

Objectives

- To revise and practise ways of generalising and distancing
- To revise collocations with *make, take, do* and *have*
- To raise awareness of speech rates and chunking when giving extended answers
- To develop a range of vocabulary related to art and artists

Before class

Make one photocopy of the worksheet on page 57, and the Rules at the end of these notes, for each group of three or four students. You will also need a set of counters and a die for each group.

❶ As a warmer Write this mini-dialogue on the board and ask students why the candidate's answer might not be appropriate for Part 3 of the IELTS Speaking test.
Examiner: Why do some people enjoy going to art galleries?
Candidate: I love art galleries. They're fantastic. All my friends hate them, though.
Explain that the candidate's answer might be regarded as too personal and too categorical. Ask students to suggest ways the answer could be improved. Elicit a range of ways of generalising and distancing (see Unit 4 of the Student's Book) and write them on the board.

> **Suggested answers**
> on the whole, generally, broadly speaking, the majority of people, seem to, tend to, have a tendency to

❷ Divide the class into groups of three or four to play the game.

❸ Explain the rules below (or give a copy to each group).

❹ Give each group a copy of the worksheet. To help students get the idea of what they are going to be doing, work through examples of each task type.

For 'Keep your distance' (grey squares), write the following question on the board: *Can people learn to be creative, or do they have to be naturally talented?* Give your own answer in around one minute (ask students to time you), using some of the strategies for generalising and distancing from the Warmer. Ask students to tell you which strategies you included.
For 'Collocation check' (white squares), write the following sentence on the board: *The majority of*

artists need to .... a profit from their work in order to survive. Ask students to complete it with *make, take, do* or *have* to make a collocation (answer: *make*). Explain that for this task type in the game, students should choose from these four verbs only.

❺ Before starting, explain that during the game, students should listen carefully to the other group members and note down any examples of what they consider to be advanced vocabulary for talking about the arts. You could also ask them to assess how well their partners 'chunk' groups of words as they speak.

> **Answers for 'Collocation check' squares**
> **2** take **5** make **8** do **10** do **14** have
> **16** make/have **19** take **25** make **28** do
> **31** have **34** make **37** take **40** do **43** have
> **46** take/have

❻ When all the groups have finished playing, ask each group to report back (constructively) on how well they managed in the areas monitored in step 5 above. Ask each group to give specific examples from their notes. At this point, you can also praise or correct any language you noticed during the game.

------------------------------✂----------------------------

Rules
1 Work in groups of three or four to play the game.
2 Take turns to play the game. Play passes to the left. When it is your turn, roll the die and move to the correct square.
3 If you land on a grey square, you must speak for at least one minute about the question. You should use as many ways as possible of generalising and distancing while you speak. Another group member will time you and tell you when your minute is up.
4 If you land on a white square, you must look carefully at the sentence decide if the missing word is *make, take, do* or *have*. Your teacher will be the referee if you disagree with the other students.
5 If you land on a black square, follow the instructions on the square.
6 If you land on a square which is already occupied by another player, or which has already been answered by another player, move forward one square.
7 The winner is the first person to reach the last square.

Unit 4 photocopiable activity
Keep your distance!

1 **START**	**2** Governments are often slow to .... action on this issue.	**3** Why do some governments not want to spend money on the arts?	**4** Miss a turn.	**5** A really good photograph can .... an instant impression.
10 The Internet could .... damage to the music industry.	**9** Move back two squares.	**8** Writers .... a lot of research before they start work.	**7** Should fashion designers be counted as artists?	**6** Move back one square.
11 Miss a turn.	**12** Move forward one square.	**13** How has the Internet affected people's access to art and design?	**14** Fashion designers .... more influence on society than painters.	**15** Move back one square.
20 Do pop stars deserve the attention they receive?	**19** Some people don't .... style into consideration when buying clothes.	**18** Miss a turn.	**17** Why might parents stop their children following a career in the arts?	**16** Making museums free would .... an impact on society.
21 Move back two squares.	**22** What makes a good photograph?	**23** Miss a turn.	**24** Should art be a hobby rather than a profession?	**25** Art therapy can really help to .... people better.
30 Should artists be allowed to say whatever they want?	**29** Move forward one square.	**28** Children who enjoy art .... better in creative tasks later on in life.	**27** Move back two squares.	**26** Should people have to pay to visit art galleries?
31 Social networking sites .... advantages for new artists.	**32** Miss a turn.	**33** How can art be used as a therapy for people with health problems?	**34** It's hard to .... predictions about the future of the music industry.	**35** Is art more important now than it used to be?
40 Pop stars always .... their best to be the centre of attention.	**39** Why do some artists choose never to show their work to others?	**38** Move forward one square.	**37** It's essential to ...... into account the role of artists in society.	**36** Move back two squares.
41 Should artists be paid more than other people?	**42** Move back two squares.	**43** Public opinion doesn't always .... an effect on government spending.	**44** Miss a turn.	**45** Should people study art from other cultures?
50 **FINISH**	**49** What effect has the Internet had on the music industry?	**48** Miss a turn.	**47** Move back two squares.	**46** Parents should encourage their children to .... an interest in art.

Word list

Unit 4

accessibility *n* [U] (42) how easy something is to understand

all shapes and sizes *phrase* (41) of many different shapes and sizes

call for something *vp* [T] (42) to need or deserve a particular action or quality

clarity *n* [U] (42) the quality of being clear and easy to understand

decorative *adj* (41) intended to be attractive rather than having a use

dogmatic *adj* (42) not willing to accept other ideas or opinions because you think yours are right

dominant *adj* (41) main or most important

durable *adj* (RS) remaining in good condition over a long time

enhance *v* [T] (48) to improve something

exert an influence *vp* [T] (42) to have an effect

format *n* [C] (41) the way something is designed, arranged or produced

foster *v* [T] (48) to encourage something to develop

give someone an opportunity *vp* [T] (41) to allow someone to have the chance to do something

grind *v* [T] (RS) to keep rubbing something between two rough, hard surfaces until it becomes a powder

in stark contrast to *phrase* (42) used to show that someone or something is completely different from someone or something else

indigenous people *np* [C] (RS) people who have lived in a place for a very long time, before other people moved to that place from different parts of the world

make advances in something *phrase* (42) to make something develop or progress

make use of something *phrase* (42) to use something that is available

meet a need for something *phrase* (43) to provide what is necessary for something

nuance *n* [C] (41) a very slight difference

override *v* [T] (48) to be more important than something else

palette *n* [C] (RS) a board used by an artist to mix their paints on while they are painting

passionate about something *adj* (RS) very enthusiastic about something

pigment *n* [C] (RS) a substance that gives something colour

prior to something *adj* (41) before something

produce *v* [T] (42) to create something

remarkable *adj* (41) very unusual or noticeable in a way that you admire

share the spotlight with something/someone *phrase* (42) to receive less attention because someone or something else has started to be noticed too

spectrum *n* [C] (41) a range of something

stimulate *v* [T] (48) to give someone the interest and excitement to do something

take advantage of something *phrase* (41) to use a situation to get something good

take hold *phrase* (41) to become popular

take off *vp* [I] (RS) to suddenly become successful

take steps to do something *phrase* (49) to take action in order to solve a problem

to this day *phrase* (41) even now, after a long period

trace *v* [T] (41) to copy a picture by putting transparent paper on top and following the outer line of the picture with a pen

a vehicle for something / doing something *phrase* (41) a way of making something happen, often a way of communicating ideas

visual art form *np* [C] (RS) something that someone has made to be beautiful or to express their ideas which can be seen, for example a painting or a sculpture

wash away *vp* [T] (RS) If water washes something away, it removes that thing.

when it comes to something / doing something *phrase* (RS) used to introduce a new idea that you want to say something about

work of art *np* [C] (40) a very beautiful and important painting, drawing, etc.

Vocabulary extension

Unit 4

abstract art *np* [U] art that involves shapes and colours, but not images of real things or people

artisan *n* [C] someone who does skilled work with their hands

award-winning design *np* [C] a design (= the planning of how a physical object will look and work) that has won prizes for its excellence

ceramic *adj* made from shaping and heating clay

conceptual art *np* [U] art which is intended mainly to express ideas and which is not intended to be beautiful in itself

contemporary *adj* of the present time

craftsmanship *n* [U] skill at making things

curator *n* [C] a person who is in charge of a museum

depict *v* [T] to represent someone or something in a picture or story

design-conscious *adj* considering design to be important

ergonomic design *np* [C/U] design which is intended to help the user of an object by being comfortable or easy to us

flourish *v* [I] to grow or develop well

functional *adj* designed to be practical and useful, not just attractive

graphic art *np* [U] art which involves drawing, painting, printing, photography, writing, etc.

industrial design *np* [U] the design that is involved in products that are for selling, and is intended to improve both their appearance and their function

innovative *adj* using new methods or ideas

interface *n* [C] a connection between two pieces of electronic equipment or between a person and a computer

offer an incentive *vp* [T] to offer something to someone that is worth having and will have the effect of making them work harder or behave in a way that you want

performing arts *plural n* types of entertainment that are performed in front of people, such as dancing, singing and acting

pottery *n* [U] plates, bowls, etc. that are made from clay

receive a government grant *vp* [T] to get an amount of money from the government for a special purpose

showcase *n* [C] an event which is intended to show the best qualities of something

state-of-the-art design *np* [U] design which uses the newest technology, ideas and materials

timeless *adj* not changing because of time or fashion

withdraw sponsorship *vp* [T] to stop providing money for an event, programme, etc. in return for advertising your own products or services

❶ Complete each of the verb + noun collocations in the sentences below using a suitable noun from the box.

condition	healing	factor	medicine	~~results~~	success	treatment

0 Exercising regularly is time-consuming, but usually yields ...*results*...

1 The placebo effect is a .... which is sometimes overlooked.

2 It takes seven years of study before you can practise ....

3 It is believed that vitamin C can promote ....

4 It is sometimes important to treat a .... before it gets worse.

5 Before patients undergo any .... , their doctor should tell them about any side effects.

6 It is difficult to gauge the .... of a drug without conducting proper clinical trials.

❷ Choose the best option for each gap.

0 The *incidence* / (*level*) of spending on healthcare varies from country to country.

1 Since anti-malarial drugs were introduced, the death *quantity* / *rate* has dropped.

2 There are several different *types* / *numbers* of drugs which can be taken to lower cholesterol.

3 The *number* / *amount* of money spent on healthcare has gone up dramatically.

4 Only a small *proportion* / *incidence* of the population develop Type 1 diabetes.

5 Having diabetes can affect every *aspect* / *type* of a person's life.

6 The *incidence* / *quantity* of heart disease is much higher in Western countries.

❸ Complete the gaps in this paragraph with the correct form of *do, have, make* or *take*.

Academics at Bristol University are **(0)** ...*taking*... action to gain legal protection for graffiti by Britain's best known graffiti artist, Banksy. Last year, cleaners **(1)** .... an expensive mistake when they scrubbed off one of his most famous pieces, *Gorilla in a Pink Mask*.

'The damage **(2)** .... by graffiti has to be **(3)** .... into consideration,' said Tom Goulding, a university lecturer, who **(4)** .... an interest in urban art, 'but work by artists such as Banksy has **(5)** .... an influence on artists worldwide. Displaying his work on our streets **(6)** .... advantages for our city.'

❹ Choose the best option (A, B or C) for each of these sentences.

0 Next year I ....*A*........ to study History of Art at university.
　(*A would like*)　　**B** like　　**C** likely

1 I wish I .... go abroad to study in Italy, but it's too expensive.
　A can　　**B** will　　**C** could

2 However, I am still .... my course.
　A expecting　　**B** looking forward to　　**C** hoping

3 When I leave university, I .... to become a professional artist.
　A dream　　**B** hope　　**C** look forward

4 This is something I have always dreamed ....
　A of　　**B** in　　**C** to do

5 However, I don't .... to make much money.
　A hope　　**B** likely　　**C** expect

5 Complete the description of the graphs below by writing a word from the box in each gap.

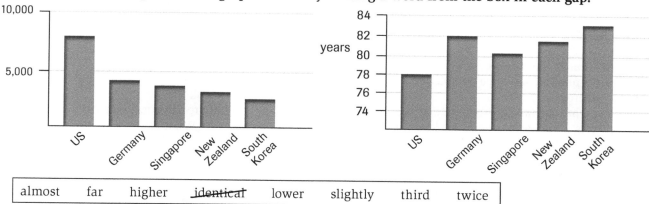

| almost | far | higher | ~~identical~~ | lower | slightly | third | twice |

The level of spending by Germany and Singapore is almost **(0)** ..i̶d̶e̶n̶t̶i̶c̶a̶l̶., at around $4,000, but life expectancy in Germany is a little **(1)** .... , at 82. However, New Zealand spends **(2)** .... less than Germany, but life expectancy is **(3)** .... the same.

The US spends more than **(4)** .... as much as New Zealand, but has a considerably **(5)** .... life expectancy, at only 78. In contrast, South Korea spends just over a **(6)** .... as much as the US, but has a **(7)** .... higher life expectancy.

6 Complete the second sentence in each pair so that it means the same as the first, using the word in brackets. Do not change the word in brackets.

0 He damaged his hand. As a result he was not able to paint. *(resulted)*
The damage to his hand ...r̶e̶s̶u̶l̶t̶e̶d̶.̶i̶n̶.̶h̶i̶s̶... not being able to paint.

1 The artist used bold colours so as to draw attention to her message. *(aim)*
The artist used bold colours with the .... attention to her message.

2 The gallery was crowded as a result of the popularity of the exhibition. *(owing)*
The gallery was crowded .... the popularity of the exhibition.

3 He inherited a Van Gogh. Consequently, he was wealthy. *(consequence)*
As a .... a Van Gogh, he was wealthy.

4 He works at night in order to be able to paint during the day. *(so)*
He works at night .... paint during the day.

5 The gallery forgot to send out the invitations, which resulted in no one attending the exhibition. *(result)*
The gallery forgot to send out the invitations, ... that no one attended the exhibition.

7 Complete each of the sentences below using a word from the box.

| claimed | ~~generally~~ | large |
| liable | rule | tend |

0 ..G̶e̶n̶e̶r̶a̶l̶l̶y̶... speaking, people are living longer these days.

1 By and .... , doctors are caring people.

2 As a .... , the more you exercise, the healthier you are.

3 Patients are .... to get annoyed if they feel their doctor is not listening to them.

4 Placebo trials .... to be more successful if a patient is treated by the same doctors.

5 It is often .... that basic healthcare should be free.

Unit 5 Stepping back in time

Unit objectives

- **Listening Section 3:** multiple choice; labelling a diagram
- **Reading Section 2:** identifying paragraph topics; matching information; sentence completion; matching features
- **Vocabulary:** word formation – negative affixes
- **Speaking Parts 2 and 3:** strategies for keeping going; giving reasons and examples
- **Pronunciation:** sentence stress 2 – showing emotion, contrasting and emphasising
- **Key grammar:** speaking hypothetically
- **Writing Task 1:** using your own words; comparing changes; organising the answer; marking stages in a process; expressing consequences and sequencing information

Starting off

❶ *As a warmer* Students work in small groups. Ask: *If you could go back in time and visit one place in your country to see what it was like, which place would it be, and why?*

- When you go through the answers, point out to students that *remains* would also fit the first gap, but that as *ruins* does not fit gap 5, the correct key is as shown below.
- *Alternative treatment* Before students complete the captions, ask them to work together and decide what each of the words in the box means. If necessary, they can use dictionaries.

> **Answers**
> 1 ruins   2 pots   3 shipwreck   4 artefacts
> 5 remains   6 burial   7 preserved   8 amber
> 9 prehistoric   10 creature

❷ *Alternative treatment* Ask students to work in pairs and just choose one of the photos.

- They should then make up a story in which they describe who might have made the discovery, what questions they might have asked about it, and what answers they might have found. (You can write these instructions on the board.)
- When they have finished, they should tell their story to another pair of students, or to the whole class.

- The students who have been listening should say whether they agree or disagree with the story and why, and ask any questions they wish.

> **Suggested answers**
> 1 builders digging foundations – What did the original city look like?
> 2 divers – What are the pots made of? / What were they used for? / What are they worth?
> 3 anyone in the area – Who owned them? / Did they have a special meaning/function?
> 4 thieves/explorers – Who/What is buried there? / What did the burial involve?
> 5 walker/farmer – What is it? / How long has it been preserved?
> 6 someone walking in the area – What prehistoric creature made the print? / When? / Is the creature now extinct?

Extension idea Ask:
- *Why do you think it's important to understand the past? In what ways does it help us to understand the present?*
- *Why is it important to teach history in schools?*

Listening   Section 3

❶ *As a warmer* Ask students: *In your culture, which do people value most: old things or new things, or both? What sort of old things would you be interested in seeing in a museum? Why?*

- Ensure students are familiar with the vocabulary from Starting off, especially *fossil*.

> **Answer**
> 2   See the diagram in Exercise 4.

Extension idea Ask students: *Why do many people think that fossils should be protected or preserved?*

❷ Remind students that they will not have time in the live exam to read and underline key ideas in the options. Also, reading the options before they listen may confuse them.

- It is more important for students to understand what they are being asked, listen for the answer and then choose the option which corresponds with what they have understood.

3 🎧 *Alternative treatment* Play the recording. Then ask students to compare their answers in pairs. Finally, they can check their answers by listening again, or reading the recording script on page 154, or both.

Answers
1 B   2 B   3 A   4 C   5 A

4 Remind students to read the rubric and check how many words they need. Also, remind them to look at the title. Impress upon them the importance of studying the diagram in the time allowed and ensuring that they have a good idea of what it shows and what they need to listen for. This task tests their ability to deal very quickly with visual material whilst listening to someone speaking.

• Ask students to:
 – compare the three diagrams
 – say how they think the process works from what they can see in the diagrams and the uncompleted labels.
• *Alternative treatment* Ask students to work alone and underline any words in the diagram where they are not sure of the meaning.
 – Ask them to work in groups and discuss what the words might mean, but do not allow them to use dictionaries (which they will not have in the exam). Tell students to use clues in the diagrams plus their own ideas to do this. Alternatively, explain the words yourself.

Answers
2 6 another word that describes the sea floor
  7 something that there is little of on the sea floor
  8 something that sediment can become
  9 something that can replace bones
 10 something like movement that can expose a fossil

5 🎧 Tell students to note down their answers as they listen. Play the recording once.
• When they have finished listening, remind them that in the live exam, they will have time to transfer their answers to the answer paper at the end.

• Tell them to complete their answers from what they have heard and, where necessary, by making intelligent guesses. Remind them that where they get an answer right, they gain a mark, but where they get an answer wrong, they will not have a mark subtracted, so it is always a good idea to make an intelligent guess when they are not sure of the answer.
• Remind them that they should also check that they have spelled their answers correctly.

Answers
6 muddy   7 oxygen   8 rock
9 minerals   10 erosion

Extension idea When students have finished, ask them to compare their answers with a partner, then play the recording again for them to check.

6 Tell students there are a number of occasions when they may have to deal with a process in the IELTS test – in the Listening section, in a Reading section labelling a diagram, and in Writing Task 1 describing a diagram – so sequencing words and phrases are generally useful.
• Go through the Language reference on page 121 with them.

Answers
2 a   3 c   4 b   5 e   6 f   7 d

7 Tell students to refer to the Language reference if they are not sure which options to choose.

Answers
1 Once   2 Whilst   3 Meanwhile
4 gradually   5 eventually   6 until

8 Give students some time to think before they discuss the questions.

Reading Section 2

1 *As a warmer* If appropriate for your class, ask students: *What makes human beings different from animals?*

2 Give students two and a half minutes to skim the passage and be strict about the timing.
• Tell students not to worry too much if they are not sure what words like *hominids* in the subheading mean. The passage may well explain these.

Answers
1 The subheading suggests that there were other species of human beside Homo sapiens, but that Homo sapiens is the only one that still survives and so is 'the last man standing'.
2 b

Extension idea Ask students to read the passage and write a note in the margin by each paragraph summarising its topic.

❸ Matching information is a typical Reading Section 2 activity and tests students' abilities to skim, scan and read in detail.

While matching headings will focus on the global idea or purpose of each paragraph, a matching-information task asks students to locate information or an idea which is embedded somewhere in one of the paragraphs. Refer students to the Exam advice box and the different types of information that may be required, for example a comparison, a reference or a mention.

- Even advanced students sometimes have problems doing this task, because they have not read the instructions carefully. They should look carefully at the instructions, as these may have some variations. If the rubric *You may use any letter more than once* is present, it means that sometimes a paragraph may contain more than one piece of information which is asked for; in other words, the same letter (A, B, C, etc.) may be used to answer more than one question. Other paragraphs may not contain any of the information required, so the letter may not be used at all. In the reading task students are asked to do here, these words are not present in the rubric. However, as there are seven paragraphs and five questions, you can point out to students, or elicit, that they will not need to use all the paragraphs.
- Ask students to look at the opening of each question, which tells them what to look for. Elicit the difference between the type of information required for Question 1 and that required for Question 2, by focusing on the opening words of the questions: *comparison* and *reference*.
- The words in the questions will not repeat words from the passage, but will contain a rephrasing or summary of an idea. For this reason, it is important to underline the key words before scanning the passage for the answers.

Suggested underlining
2 reference / items / trade
3 mention / evidence / unknown human species
4 mention / ill fortune / downfall / Neanderthal
5 reference / final / location / Neanderthals

❹ Remind students that, by the nature of the task, they will not find the information in the passage in the same order as the questions, hence the need to study the questions fairly carefully before scanning the passage; this will enable them to recognise the information more readily when they are reading.

Answers
1 D (*Both species were strong and stockier than the average human today … Homo sapiens, on the other hand, had longer forearms …*)
2 E (*Objects such as shell beads and flint tools … in order to barter and exchange useful materials, and share ideas and knowledge.*)
3 A (*Meanwhile, an unusual finger bone and tooth … have led scientists to believe that yet another human population – the Denisovans – may also have been widespread across Asia.*)
4 G (*During each rapid climate fluctuation, they may have suffered greater losses of people than Homo sapiens, and thus were slowly worn down,' he says.*)
5 C (*… the Neanderthals … eventually disappeared from the landscape around 30,000 years ago, with their last known refuge being southern Iberia, including Gibraltar.*)

❺ The aim of the sentence-completion task is to test students' ability to skim and scan to find the relevant part of the passage and then to read in detail to answer the questions.

- They need not read the whole passage again carefully; they can use key words or key ideas within the question to locate the relevant part of the passage and read that part carefully.
- Remind students that names or proper nouns are always likely to be key words, as these cannot be paraphrased.
- Before students answer the questions, remind them to copy the words they need exactly from the passage and to read the sentence through to check that it makes sense and is grammatical.
- When they have finished, they can compare their answers with a partner.
- When rounding up with the class, ask why skulls would not be a correct answer to Question 9 (*answer*: because *skulls* is not the exact word in the passage). Also ask them how they knew they had to produce a three-word answer for Question 7 (*answer*: because of the word *both*).
- ***Alternative treatment*** If you want to give them an experience of exam pressure, give them five minutes to answer the questions.

Answers

1 *Suggested underlining*

  6 stone tools / Petraglia's / Homo sapiens / eastern India

  7 Homo sapiens / both / sewing

  8 territorial / Neanderthals / resources

  9 Neanderthal / language and thought

2 6 something similar to or related to tools

  7 two materials used to make sewing implements

  8 something in addition to resources that Neanderthals failed to get

  9 something related to language and thought

4 6 (dating) sediment layers (*Based on careful examination of the tools and dating of the sediment layers where they were found, Petraglia and his team suggest that Homo sapiens arrived in eastern India around 78,000 years ago …* (paragraph B))

  7 ivory and bone / bone and ivory (*Archaeologists have uncovered simple needles fashioned from ivory and bone, alongside Homo sapiens …* (paragraph D))

  8 (new) technologies (*They misdirected their energies by only gathering resources from their immediate surroundings and perhaps failing to discover new technologies outside their territory.* (paragraph E))

  9 skull shapes (*By comparing skull shapes, …* (paragraph F))

❻ The matching-features task tests students' ability to scan the passage for options (in this case, names of researchers) and then read that part of the passage carefully to find the information or opinion which goes with each name.

- Draw students' attention to the instructions and the form of the task. Point out that, as there are four questions but only three researchers, they will have to use one researcher twice. Tell them:
  - they should underline key ideas in the questions to focus on exactly what is being asked, although the ideas will be expressed in the passage using different words
  - there will not, in this case, be a researcher (or other option) listed who (or which) they do not have to use
  - it is always important to note the number of questions and the number of options (in this case, names). Here, they will need to use one letter twice. Other times, the box may contain more options than the number of questions and in that case, they will not need to use all the letters

- they should then scan to locate where the options occur in the passage and read carefully from there
- the same name or option may occur in different places in the passage, and they should scan the passage for all instances
- the names are listed in the same order as in their first occurrence in the passage.

Answers

1 *Suggested underlining*

  10 No evidence / Neanderthal / allocated tasks

  11 Homo sapiens / plan ahead

  12 Scientists cannot be sure / natural disaster / loss / human species

  13 Environmental conditions restricted / Homo sapiens / Neanderthals / live

3 10 C ('*We see similar kinds of injuries on male and female Neanderthal skeletons, implying there was no such division of labour,*' says Spikins.)

  11 B (*We think that Homo sapiens had a significantly more complex language than Neanderthals and were able to comprehend and discuss concepts such as the distant past and future,*' says Stringer.)

  12 A (… *says Petraglia. 'Whether the eruption of Toba also played a role in the extinction of the Homo erectus-like species is unclear to us.*')

  13 B (*But then Europe's climate swung into a cold, inhospitable, dry phase. 'Neanderthal and Homo sapiens populations had to retreat to refugia (pockets of habitable land). This heightened competition between the two groups,' explains Chris Stringer …*).

❼ *Alternative treatment* Use the questions for a general class discussion.

Vocabulary Word formation – negative affixes

❶ *As a warmer* Write these 'wrong' words on the board: *dissatisfied, uncompetent, inforgettable, unecessary, non-correct.*

- Tell students that all the words are somehow wrong. Ask them to work in pairs and correct them (*answers*: dissatisfied, incompetent, unforgettable, unnecessary, incorrect).
- When students have done the exercise, go through the Language reference on page 114 with them. Refer them particularly to the spelling rules, as this is a major area of error.

Answers

1 disappeared   2 inhospitable

3 misdirected   4 unstable

Extension idea Ask students to say what the words they have used to fill the gaps mean and how the prefix has changed the meaning (*disappear* – *appear* means 'to start to be seen', but *disappear* in this context means 'to stop existing'; *inhospitable* – *hospitable* means, in this context, that the climate provided good conditions for living, but *inhospitable* means the opposite; *misdirected* – *directed* means 'aimed' or 'used', but *misdirected* means they used or aimed (their energies) in a wrong way; *unstable* – *stable* means 'unlikely to move or change', but *unstable*, in this context, means it changed frequently and therefore was not safe).

❷ Ask students to refer to the Language reference when they do this exercise, particularly to check that they are spelling their answers correctly.
- Remind them that they may have to make more changes than simply adding a negative affix: for example, they may have to add a suffix to change a base word from a verb to an adjective, etc.

Answers
2 disorganised   3 worthless   4 irreplaceable
5 illogical   6 non-existent   7 underestimated
8 impractical   9 degraded   10 illiterate

Extension idea Ask students to use their dictionaries to check:
- their answers
- what each word means.

❸ *Alternative treatment* Ask students to write their answers.
- When they have finished, they can read them out to the whole class, who then say whether they agree or disagree with them and why.

Suggested answers
2 ... scientists misinterpret the data.
3 ... the ageing process is irreversible.
4 ... they may be disorganised in their work/home life.
5 ... many of the items they display are irreplaceable.

Speaking   Parts 2 and 3

❶ *As a warmer* In small groups and with books closed, remind students that when they do Part 2, they have one minute to think and make notes before they start. Ask them to discuss: *How do you make notes for this? What should you write, and how do you use them?*
- Round up ideas with the whole class, then refer them to Tibah's notes and the questions.

Suggested answer
1   They are a list of ideas and vocabulary connected with the prompts, but not organised. They may help her to keep going and use suitable vocabulary.

Extension idea Ask: *How do these notes compare with the notes you make?* What sort of notes work best for you?
You can suggest that noting down suitable advanced-level vocabulary is a useful way to prepare.

❷ 🎧

Suggested answer
She uses them to suggest vocabulary and prompt her to keep going. She doesn't mention all her ideas in the same order as on the prompt card.

❸ 🎧 *Alternative treatment* Ask students to suggest phrases to complete the extracts before they listen again. This needn't be a memory task, but if they remember what Tibah said, they can use those phrases.

Answers
2 tell you   3 far as   4 my mother   5 wouldn't say
6 eye-catching   7 having said

Extension ideas
1   Ask students to work in small groups and brainstorm other phrases they could use for each of the strategies.
- When they have finished, round up with the whole class and write the most useful ones on the board.
- Ask students to note them in their notebooks.
2   Ask students to look at the recording script on page 156. Then ask them to work in pairs and find examples of (you can write these on the board):
- *relative clauses*
- *phrases giving reasons*
- *conditional sentences*
- *phrases expressing purpose*
- *a quote of someone's actual words.*
- Draw students' attention to the length of sentences and the variety of structures used, and point out that these will help Tibah achieve a very high band score for this task in the exam.

Suggested answers
1   a full introduction: *I'm going to talk about, The thing I'd like to talk about* ... picking the point she can say most about: *I'll start off by talking about ..., I'd like to start by saying ...*

speculates: *it could have come from ..., It may have been acquired ...*

includes a saying: *as you often hear ...*

what the item is not: *It's certainly not ...*

compares: *it's much more valuable than ... whereas ... is ... this is ...*

concession: *however, although*

2 relative clauses: *that I could talk about, that I keep in my attic, who was 95 years old, who'd bought it in a market in India, that has sentimental value, you'd choose to put on, that are quite chipped and faded now, that I got for my 21st birthday*

phrases giving reasons: *so it's hard for me to decide what to choose, because ... I don't wear them*

conditional sentences: *if I were to lose it, I'd be really upset; You wouldn't realise how old it was unless you examined it closely, If I were to throw the beads out, I wouldn't be able to forgive myself, if it hadn't been for my granny's aunt, I wouldn't have inherited that necklace*

phrases expressing purpose: *so that they become an equally important family treasure*

a quote of someone's actual words: *'you can't put a price on something that has sentimental value'*

Note: this would be a good time to do the Key grammar section on speaking hypothetically.

4 When students give their talks, keep track of the time and ask them to keep talking for the full two minutes. Tell them they should speak until you say 'thank you'.

- **Alternative treatment** Elicit and write this short checklist on the board, and ask students to use it to give feedback to their partners on their talks.
  Did your partner:
  – *use a range of advanced-level vocabulary?*
  – *keep going for the full two minutes?*
  – *deal with all the points on the prompt card?*
  – *introduce and round off their talk?*

5 Point out to students that there are really two parts to this question which they must deal with and that they can suggest several ideas for each part. This will produce a long answer.

6 Elicit why it is important to give reasons and examples in answers. (*Answer:* They validate or support what the speaker is saying, making the answer more persuasive. In the IELTS test, it is a good strategy to give longish answers, as this allows students to demonstrate a range of vocabulary, grammatical structure, coherence and fluency – giving reasons and examples is the obvious way to do this.)

Answers

1 memories; with photographs

2

reasons	examples
I think that's the main reason why ...	Perhaps the most obvious example of this is ...
I'm sure there are all sorts of reasons, but perhaps the main one is ...	You know, ...
I think it must be a question of ...	By that I mean ...

7 **Answers**

1 See table above.

2 Both Johannes, who talks about people who keep old things and people who don't, and Margarete, who talks about space available, give good answers.

8 Remind students that it is important to pay careful attention to the question that is being asked and to try to answer it as exactly as possible; if there is more than one part to the question, take time answering both/all parts.

Note: this would be a good time to do the Pronunciation section.

9 *Alternative treatment 1* Ask students:
– *In which questions will you have to make some comparisons?* (*answer:* in the first, second and possibly sixth questions)
– *Which questions will you need to talk about the future?* (*answer:* in the third and sixth questions)

- *Alternative treatment 2* Before students ask and answer the questions, elicit and write this checklist on the board:
  Did your partner:
  – *answer all aspects of the question?*
  – *give a fairly long answer?*
  – *include reasons and examples?*
  – *use stress effectively to emphasise particular points?*

Encourage students to use it to evaluate their partners while they speak.

Pronunciation Sentence stress 2

1 *As a warmer* Write on the board: *Johannes gives a complete answer, but Kenny only gives a partial answer.* If necessary, refer students back to the question that Johannes and Kenny are answering (Exercise 5 on page 58) for context.

- Ask students: *If you were speaking, which words would you stress, and why?* (*Suggested answer:*

Johannes / complete / Kenny, partial – these are the words which emphasise the comparison or contrast between the two pieces of information and carry the purpose of the sentence.)

- Draw students' attention to the introduction to this section. On the board, add this sentence to the one above: *That means that Johannes will get a higher mark.*
- Ask why *That* is stressed (*answer:* it is highlighting a reference back to the previous sentence).
- You can point out that if the sentence was *It means that Johannes will get a higher mark, It* would not be stressed, as it is a non-emphatic reference.
- ⌒ *Alternative treatment* Play the recording of Johannes's answer again (Track 1.29) while students read the answer.

Extension idea Ask students in pairs to read Johannes's answer aloud to each other.

> **Answers**
> *that* – a (reference back to *personality*)
> *some/other* – c
> *really* – b (to emphasise *sentimental*)
> *even though* – c (to highlight linker used for contrast)
> *were* – b (to stress inversion and show emphatic use of conditional)
> *loss* – b
> *they're* – a (to refer back to *other people*)
> *present* – b

❷

> **Answers**
> 1/2 *memories* – b (to highlight word)
> *that's* – a (to refer back to opening to answer)
> *main* – b
> *keep* – b
> *obvious* – b
> *photographs* – b
> *might* – b
> *themselves* – c (as opposed to the ones they like other aspects of)
> *keep* – a (to contrast with *get rid of*)
> *remind* – b
> *person/event* – b

❸ Ask students to write two or three sentences (in other words, to give longish answers, as they would do in the exam).

❹ *Extension idea* Ask students to change partners and ask and answer the questions in Exercise 3 without reading, as they would do in the exam. Tell them this is to practise using sentence stress more naturally and spontaneously.

Key grammar Speaking hypothetically

❶ *As a warmer* Write on the board:
- a *If he sold the house, he'd be quite wealthy.*
- b *If he had sold the house, he'd have been quite wealthy.*
- c *If he had sold the house, he'd be quite wealthy.*
- Ask students: *What is the difference in meaning between the three sentences?* (*Answers:* a) refers to the present or future, b) to the past, and c) to the past in the first half and the present in the second half.)
- Point out to students that there are a number of variants to conditional constructions, which they will be working on in this section.
- ⌒ *Alternative treatment* Ask students to check their answers by listening to Tibah again (Track 1.28).

> **Answers**
> 1 if   2 unless   3 were   4 for; have

❷ Tell or remind students that it is possible to combine second and third conditionals in one sentence, depending on whether each part of the sentence refers to the present or the past.
- Remind them that the second conditional refers to a hypothetical present or future, and the third conditional refers to a past that did not happen and therefore is also hypothetical.
- When they have done the exercise, go through the Language reference on page 118 with them.

> **Answers**
> 1 c   2 a   3 a   4 b

❸ > **Answers**
> 1 didn't touch / did not touch   2 to fall
> 3 would have reached   4 had had
> 5 would never have found
> 6 was opened   7 had known   8 not been

❹ Remind students that they will achieve a higher band score using complex sentences and advanced grammar appropriately. The grammar they have been studying in this section is suitable for both the Speaking and the Writing papers.
- *Alternative treatment* Ask students to work alone and write their answers to each question. They then compare and discuss their answers in small groups.

Suggested answers

1 … we would have reached the top of the mountain.
2 … we could live somewhere like that.
3 … I'd have to go back to college.
4 … I wouldn't have been able to afford to buy my flat.
5 … I should be able to go on holiday this summer.
6 … I told my parents where I was going and when I would be back.

Writing Task 1

❶ *As a warmer* With books closed, ask students to work in small groups. Ask them: *When do you look at diagrams to help you do things or understand things? When are diagrams more helpful than words?*

- Remind students that it is essential they use their own words when writing the task. Phrases lifted from the task to their answers without any modification will not be counted and thus lower their band score.
- Tell them that examiners will check that all the key stages are covered in their description of a process, so it is essential to identify the stages which need describing before they start.
- *Alternative treatment* Elicit synonyms for these words: *illustrates* (shows, explains); *were exposed* (were uncovered, were revealed, were brought to the surface); *beneath* (below, underneath, under, at the bottom of); *coastal* (by the sea, on the coast)

Suggested answers

1 It shows how the changes in a cliff face revealed fossil remains.
2 a The action of the sea, the changing position of the cliff, the erosion and exposure of fossils.
   b Changes in the position and shape of the cliff; the tides and the level of the seawater; the sea floor/base and the rocks/stones
   c Coastline, stones, rocks, tide, waves, power, force, expose, reveal, retreat, erode, etc.
3 According to the stages in the diagram
4 A summary of the impact of erosion

❷ *Alternative treatment* Before they order the sentences, ask students to match each sentence to part of the diagram or, in the case of the introductory sentence and the overview, to the whole diagram.

- Ask them to underline words and phrases in the sentences which refer to other sentences, or other parts of the answer (*Conversely, Meanwhile, As a result, As the waves hit, these waves, this meant*). Remind students that using words and phrases like these gives the answer coherence and therefore a higher band score.

Answer

e, h, a, g, c, f, b, d

The diagram shows the changes that took place in a cliff face as a result of coastal erosion, and how this led to the discovery of fossils.

At one time, the cliff stood much further out and, at low tide, the sea water did not touch the base of the rock. Conversely, at high tide, the waves sometimes reached half-way up the cliff wall, beating on it with some force.

Eventually, the power of these waves loosened and wore away the rock. This meant that stones and boulders fell into the sea, and the cliff slowly retreated, exposing previously buried rock at low tide.

As the waves hit the lower part of the cliff more frequently, this area eroded more quickly and became a hollow in the cliff wall where fossils could be found. Meanwhile, the overhanging cliff at the top cracked, creating a dangerous area beneath it.

Clearly, the fossils would have remained buried and the coastline unchanged if it had not been for the action of the sea.

❸ Elicit why using words and phrases to mark the stages, i.e. sequencers, is important. (*Answer:* It helps the reader to follow the process clearly.)

- Ask students to look back to the words and phrases like these that they worked on in the Listening section on page 54.

Answers

a as a result / At one time / Eventually / As
b Conversely / Meanwhile

Extension ideas

1 Ask students to suggest other words and phrases which can be used to mark stages in a process (some possibilities: *in the past, finally, in consequence, while, in the meantime, on the other hand*). Write the most useful ones on the board for students to copy into their notebooks.
2 Ask students to write a brief description of the process they follow when doing an IELTS Writing task. When they have finished, they can exchange their descriptions with a partner and compare their use of sequencers.

❹ Tell students that this is one use of participle clauses and that they are not used just to express consequences. (They may, for example, substitute relative clauses as in *People living and working in cities are prone to higher levels of stress than people living in the country*, or they may substitute time clauses as in *Living in the country, he met his wife*.)

- When students have finished the exercise, go through the Language reference on page 121 with them.

Answers
1 the waves reaching half-way up the cliff wall
2 The participle clause is separated by a comma.
3 *exposing previously buried rock at low tide* (the cliff retreating from its position)
   creating a dangerous area beneath it (the cracking of the overhanging cliff)

❺ **Answers**
1 ... science, transforming our ability ...
2 ... CT-scanned, revealing ...
3 ... rock, making it hard ...
4 ... beach, carrying the sand ...
5 ... cliff wall, producing ...

Extension idea Ask students to write two sentences of their own expressing consequences using participle clauses. When they have finished, they should read out their sentences to the whole class.

❻ Point out or elicit that the task here supplies information in general about headlands, whereas the task in Exercise 1 showed information about a particular instance of how fossils were revealed. As a consequence, when answering this question, present tenses are more suitable.
- ***Alternative treatment*** Brainstorm useful vocabulary with the whole class and write it on the board. Ask students to work in pairs and:
  - decide what is happening in the process, and how they would describe the key stages
  - decide what comparisons they can make
  - write an introductory sentence using their own words as far as possible
  - decide what they can say as an overview.

❼ Students can do the Writing task for homework. However, remind them to look back through the unit for language they have studied which might be useful here.
- Tell them to spend a maximum of 20 minutes on the task, including planning and checking.

Sample answer
The four pictures illustrate the changes that can take place in the appearance of a headland as a result of coastal erosion.
A headland is a cliff or large rock that extends into the sea. Initially, it is solid, but over time, the movement of the sea water can wear away a weak part at the base of the rock, to form a small hollow or cave. At high tide, the water may reach half-way up the headland and gradually the motion of the

waves can widen the cave, turning it into an arch. Durdle Door in Dorset is an example of this type of erosion.
As the water continually beats against the arch, it can weaken the top part, which eventually collapses, leaving an isolated piece of rock called a 'stack'. Over time, the stack also wears away to form a 'stump'. Meanwhile, more caves may develop along the base of the headland, and additional arches and stacks can be created.
The diagrams clearly show how the continual process of erosion, with the formation of caves, arches and stumps of rock, contributes to the eventual withdrawal of a headland.

Extension idea Give students a deadline for doing the Writing task. When they bring their answers to class, ask them to work in small groups and exchange answers. Ask them to check the following things (which you can write on the board):
Have they:
- *written an introductory sentence using their own words?*
- *described all the main stages?*
- *introduced the different stages using suitable sequencers?*
- *used participle clauses to express consequences?*
- *made some comparisons?*
- *divided their answer into paragraphs?*
- *included an overview?*
They should then give each other feedback and make any changes to their answers before handing them in to you.

Unit 5 photocopiable activity
Heating through history Time: 60 minutes

Objectives

- To practise the use of sequencers when describing processes
- To practise using participle clauses to express consequences
- To revise and practise language for speaking hypothetically
- To check the use and spelling of negative affixes
- To develop proofreading skills in preparation for exam writing

Before class

Make one photocopy of the worksheet on page 72 for each student.

❶ As a warmer Ask students: *How are your homes heated? What kind of heating systems do you think existed 2,000 years ago? How do you imagine homes in the future will be heated?*

❷ Give each student a copy of the worksheet. Focus students on Diagram 1 and the sample answer on the worksheet. Point out that the answer contains a number of mistakes.

❸ Put students in A/B pairs. Focus their attention on the words in bold in the sample answer.
Get Student A to find:
a   two errors in the use of sequencers
b   two errors in the use of negative prefixes.
Get Student B to find:
c   one place where the writer could have used a participle clause to express purpose, but did not
d   an error in the use of language for speaking hypothetically.
They then report back to their partners with details of the errors they have found and suggestions for correcting them. Line numbers are given for ease of reference.

❹ Conduct a feedback session with the whole class, going through the answers and responding to any queries.

Suggested answers

a   *While* (line 4) cannot be used at the start of a sentence. *Meanwhile* would be suitable here. *Until* (line 6) should be replaced with *As* or *While*.
b   ~~undirectly~~ indirectly (line 6); ~~dissappeared~~ disappeared (line 8)
c   … which were built into the bathroom walls, providing a further source of heat for the bathroom. (lines 6–7)
d   Had these not been used, the heat ~~had not been~~ **would not have been** able to circulate freely. (line 5)

❺ Focus students on Diagram 2. Tell them to write their own answers to the second task in at least 150 words. Give a time limit of 20 minutes. When writing, students should pay special attention to accuracy in the areas discussed in steps 3 and 4 above. They should also try to use at least one participle clause to express consequences.

❻ When they have finished writing, encourage them to swap answers with their partner and check carefully, paying particular attention to comparative grammar, sequencers, affixes and participle clauses.

Extension idea Students do some research of their own to find out about a technical process which existed in ancient times, such as ship building, weaving or cooking with ovens. This could lead to a short presentation to the rest of the class, in which each student describes the process involved, with the aid of a diagram.

Heating through history

Diagram 1

The diagram on the right illustrates a system designed by the Ancient Romans to heat the bathroom in a villa.
Summarise the information by selecting and reporting the main features, and make comparisons where relevant.

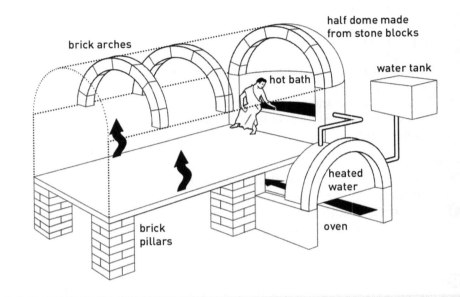

brick arches

half dome made from stone blocks

hot bath

water tank

heated water

brick pillars

oven

Sample answer

The diagram shows the heating system in the bathroom of an ancient Roman villa.

An underground furnace was used to heat water in a tank, which was fed by a water cistern higher up. The heated water was transferred directly from the tank into a hot bath in the bathing area.

While, hot air and gases from the furnace passed under the floor of the bathroom, which was positioned on top of brick pillars.
5 Had these not been used, the heat **had not been** able to circulate freely. Thus, the whole area of the bathroom was heated **undirectly** from below. **Until** the hot air rose, it passed through special pipes called flues, which were built into the bathroom walls. **This provided** a further source of heat for the bathroom.

Eventually, the hot air passed through the flues and **dissappeared** through the ceiling, by means of hollow brick ribs positioned inside the bathroom roof.

10 The system was designed to make maximum use of the heat from the furnace, functioning both as a water heater and as a central-heating system.

Diagram 2

The diagram on the right shows a solar water-heating system from a contemporary home.
Summarise the information by selecting and reporting the main features, and make comparisons where relevant.

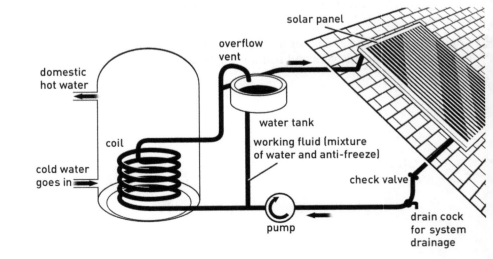

solar panel

overflow vent

domestic hot water

water tank

working fluid (mixture of water and anti-freeze)

coil

cold water goes in

check valve

pump

drain cock for system drainage

Word list

Unit 5

allocate *v* [T] (56) If you allocate a task to someone, you give them that particular task.

artefacts *plural n* [C] (52) objects, especially very old objects, of historical interest

barter *v* [I/T] (55) to exchange goods or services for other goods or services, without using money

be a question of something *phrase* (59) to be related to something

burial site *np* [C] (52) an area of land where dead bodies are buried

catch up on something *vp* [T] (53) to do something that you did not have time to do earlier

erode *v* [I/T] (61) If soil, stone, etc. erodes or is eroded, it is gradually damaged and removed by the sea, rain or wind.

coastal erosion *np* [U] (60) the gradual disappearance of cliffs, beaches, etc. as a result of the action of the sea

come about *vp* [I] (55) to happen or start to happen

compact *v* [T] (RS) to press something together so that it becomes tight or solid

current *n* [C] (54) the natural flow of water in one direction

die out *vp* [I] (54) to become more and more rare and then disappear completely

division of labour *singular n* (55) a way of organising work so that different people are responsible for different tasks

entomb *v* [T] (RS) to bury something or someone in something so they cannot escape

exceptionally *adv* (60) unusually

fault lines *plural n* (RS) breaks in the Earth's surface

fossilisation *n* [U] (RS) the process of becoming a fossil (= part of an animal or plant from many thousands of years ago, preserved in rock)

give someone or something the edge *phrase* (55) to give someone an advantage over someone else

heritage *n* [U] (54) the buildings, paintings, customs, etc. which are important in a culture or society because they have existed for a long time

immediate surroundings *plural n* (55) Your immediate surroundings are the area that is closest to you.

implement *n* [C] (55) a tool

imply *v* [T] (55) to suggest or show something

inheritance *n* [C/U] (58) money or possessions that you get from someone when they die

an insight into something *np* [C] (56) a way of understanding what something is really like

keep themselves to themselves *phrase* (55) If a group of people keep themselves to themselves, they stay with that group and do not spend time with other people.

lead someone to do something *vp* (54) to cause someone to do or think something

lessen *v* [I/T] (55) to become less, or to make something less

lobe *n* [C] (55) one of the parts of the brain

maintain links with something *phrase* (59) to keep a connection with something

mimic *v* [T] (RS) to have the same behaviour or qualities as something else

plummet *v* [I] (55) If an amount or level of something plummets, it suddenly becomes very much lower.

predator *n* [C] (RS) an animal that kills and eats other animals

refuge *n* [C] (55) a place where you are protected from danger

robust *adj* (55) strong and thick

sediment *n* [C/U] (53) a layer of sand, stones, etc. that eventually forms a layer of rock

sentimental value *n* [U] (RS) importance that an object has because it makes you remember someone or something and not because it is worth a lot of money

silt *n* [U] (54) sand and clay that has been carried along by a river and is left on land

stocky *adj* (55) having a wide, strong body

trait *n* [C] (55) a quality in someone's character

turn the clock back *phrase* (55) to go back in time

wear away *vp* [I/T] (61) to disappear after a lot of time or use, or to make something disappear in this way

wear someone/something down *vp* [T] (55) to make someone or something gradually lose their strength

widespread *adj* (55) existing in a lot of places

Vocabulary extension

Unit 5

archaeological remains *plural n* the parts of ancient societies that are left, usually in the ground, when everything else has disappeared or been destroyed

ancient monument *n* [C] a building or other structure from a very long time ago

belong to a period *vp* to come from a particular time

buried underground *phrase* If something is buried underground, it has been put under the surface of the ground.

carbon dating *n* [U] a method of calculating the age of extremely old objects by measuring the amount of a particular type of carbon in them

chronological *adj* arranged in the order in which events happened

date back to *vp* [T] If something dates back to a particular period or year, it has existed since then.

decay *v* [I] to gradually become bad or weak or be destroyed, often because of natural causes, such as bacteria or age

demography *n* [U] the study of the characteristics of people in a particular area

ethnic origins *plural n* the race that someone comes from

find *n* [C] something valuable, interesting or useful that is discovered

fragment *n* [C] a small piece from something bigger

intricately carved *phrase* cut with many small details

invisible to the naked eye *phrase* unable to be seen without special equipment

irreversible damage *np* [U] harm that cannot be removed or repaired

mammoth *n* [C] a type of large elephant with hair and tusks that no longer exists

medieval *adj* relating to the period in Europe between about AD 500 and AD 1500

on the shoreline *phrase* on the edge of a sea, lake or big river

palaeontologist *n* [U] someone who studies fossils as a way of getting information about the history of life on Earth and the structure of rocks

prehistoric creature *np* [C] an animal or bird from a time long ago before there were written records

relic *n* [C] a very old thing from the past

remote area *np* [C] an area that is a long way from any towns or cities

reveal *v* [T] to allow something to be seen that, until then, had been hidden

settlement *n* [C] a town or village that people built to live in after arriving from somewhere else

sunken vessel *np* [C] a ship or large boat that has sunk below the surface of the water

tomb *n* [C] a place where a dead person is buried, usually with a monument (= stone structure)

unearth *v* [T] to find something in the ground

well-preserved *adj* still in good condition and not very damaged by age

weathered *adj* looking rough and old

Unit 6 IT society

Starting off

❶ *As a warmer* With books closed, ask students in small groups to think of all the screens they might look at in a day (for example: a TV screen, a computer screen) and what they use them for.

> **Answers**
> 1 d 2 b 3 e 4 f 5 c 6 a

❷ For 3e, elicit the answer from the whole class. (*Suggested answer:* In the past, people used to queue in the bank and then talk to a cashier to do simple financial transactions. Now they can do this from home at any time of day.)
- Remind students that *used to* is a useful verb for talking about things people generally did in the past but do not do now. Students can use the present perfect to say how things have changed.

Extension idea Ask: *Which of these inventions has made the most difference to the way we live? What downsides do these technologies have?*

❸ When students have finished, ask them to report back to the whole class.

Extension idea
Ask students to work in pairs and think of and prepare a short talk on another area of life which they think IT will change in the future.
- When they are ready, ask them to change partners and take turns to give their talks.

Reading Section 3

❶ *As a warmer* Ask students in small groups: *Which subjects is it essential for all children to study at school?* Ask students to draw up a list.

Extension idea Ask students to discuss in pairs:
- *How much do you use the maths you studied at school in your daily life?*
- *Which areas of maths do you find most useful?*

❷ Remind students that before reading, they should always check the title, subheading and any illustrations which are intended to help them.
- *Alternative treatment* Tell students that in the live exam, they should also quickly check which reading tasks they will have to do with the passage. Ask them to check the ones which go with this one (*answers:* multiple choice, Yes / No / Not Given, matching sentence endings).

> **Suggested answer**
> Something about Khan Academy, and about the use of visual/interactive materials in school and how this is changing teaching methods

Extension idea If students have heard about Khan Academy, ask them what they already know about it and its methods.

❸ The questions in this exercise are intended to guide students' skimming, so they should give brief general answers.
- Give students a maximum of three minutes for this skimming task and be strict about the time limit.
- Tell them not to write their answers – they don't have time – but when they have finished, ask them to compare their answers in pairs.

> **Answers**
> Khan Academy is an educational website (containing 2,400 videos on maths) that students can watch at home or teachers can use in classrooms. It is changing the way maths is taught and the way students learn. Teachers and students like it, but some educationalists are critical of it.

4 Tell students that often IELTS questions require them to understand an idea or information expressed across more than one sentence and that writers often link these ideas together using reference word/phrases.

- *Alternative treatment* Ask students to find words/phrases in the first paragraph which refer to things in other parts of the paragraph (*his, him, he* – the fifth grader; *It's* – the math problem; *it* – the problem; *ten* – ten problems).

Answers
2 an educational website
3 a video
4 Thordarson's normal instruction
5 one-to-one instruction
6 overhauling the school curricula
7 Khan's fans
8 schools becoming test-prep factories
9 the lecture

5 Tell, or elicit from, students that the best technique for dealing with multiple-choice questions is to:
- underline the key ideas in the question first (but not read options A–D)
- find the relevant part of the passage, read and understand it
- read options A–D and choose the one which matches with what they have understood
- finally, underline the words in the passage which support their choice of answer (if there are no words supporting their choice, the answer will be wrong).
- Tell students that answers will be found in the same order in the passage as in the questions, so when they scan for the next question, they do not need to start from the beginning each time.
- Remind students that the questions will paraphrase words and ideas in the passage, but probably not use the same words, so they should be wary of options which repeat words from the passage, unless the words are names or terms that cannot easily be rephrased.
- When students have finished, point out that it is essential to understand what *it* (in *work it out*) refers to in order to answer Question 1.

Suggested underlining
2 content / Khan Academy videos
3 *this reversal* / line 40
4 teaching / 'middle' / class
5 Students praise / videos / because

Answers
1 D ("*It took a while for me to work it out,*" …)
2 B (*… they consist of a voiceover by the site's founder, Salman Khan, chattily describing a mathematical concept or explaining how to solve a problem, while his hand-scribbled formulas and diagrams appear on-screen.*)
3 C (*This involves replacing some of her lectures with Khan's videos, which students can watch at home.*)
4 B (*Schools have spent millions of dollars on sophisticated classroom technology, but the effort has been in vain.*)
5 D (*… steps that teachers often gloss over.*)

6 Remind students that, like True / False / Not Given tasks, each question in Yes / No / Not Given tasks will contain key words which are the same as or similar to words in the passage, so they should identify these key words and then scan the passage until they find them. Once located, they should read that part of the passage carefully, bearing in mind that even if a question has the answer Not Given, the topic of the question will be treated in the passage.

- When students have finished underlining, point out that it is essential to understand what *that* (in *far more than that*) refers to in order to answer Question 6 (see key below) and what *so* (in *for doing so*) refers to for Question 7.

Suggested underlining
6 Thordarson's first impressions / Khan Academy / wrong
7 Khan / change / courses
8 grade levels / progressing / different rates
9 principals / invited Khan / schools
10 Khan / advice / start-up projects

Answers
6 YES (*Initially, Thordarson thought Khan Academy would merely be a helpful supplement to her normal instruction. But it quickly became far more than that.*)
7 NO (*Khan never intended to overhaul the school curricula and he doesn't have a consistent, comprehensive plan for doing so.*)
8 NO (*The very concept of grade levels implies groups of students moving along together at an even pace.*)
9 NOT GIVEN (Principals are mentioned, but there is nothing about them inviting Khan into their schools.)
10 NOT GIVEN (Start-ups are mentioned, but there is nothing about Khan giving advice on them.)

❼ Matching sentence endings tests students' ability to scan the passage for words relating to each sentence beginning and then to understand in detail what is said, before matching the idea or information with a paraphrased ending.

In the task in this unit, all of the sentence beginnings contain names, so clearly students should scan the passage for the names and then carefully read what each person says.

- Remind students to read and understand what the relevant part of the passage says first, before they read the options. If they do this, they are likely to answer both more quickly and more accurately.

Suggested underlining
11 Bill Gates thinks
12 Gary Stager
13 Sylvia Martinez regrets
14 Ben Kamens / told
Answers
11 B (*Nevertheless, some of his fans believe that he has stumbled onto the solution to education's middle-of-the-class mediocrity. Most notable among them is Bill Gates, …*)
12 D (*Schools have become "joyless test-prep factories," he says, and Khan Academy caters to this dismal trend.*)
13 G (*… she doubts that it would work for the majority of pupils …*)
14 E (*… wondered whether they could modify it "to stop students from becoming this advanced."*)

❽ *Extension ideas*
1 Ask students to work in small groups and discuss: *What are the advantages and disadvantages of distance learning?*
2 If you have not already done so, refer students to online resources which help students prepare for IELTS, such as www.ielts.org and www.cambridgeesol.org/exams/ielts/index.html .

Listening Section 4

❶ *As a warmer* With books closed, ask students in small groups to discuss how IT has affected the film industry. If any of them are stuck for ideas, you can suggest some of the following areas: the technology of making films, especially special effects, cameras and digital technology, distribution of films, markets for DVDs, online piracy, etc.

- If students have difficulty producing ideas for the questions in the book, mention some of the ideas in the suggested answers below to get them started.

Suggested answers
1 They had to do everything by hand. / It required many drawings. / Artists were required with excellent skills.
2 Children love the colours / expressions / animal characters, etc.
For adults, there is a lot of humour that they can appreciate / animated films can stir many different emotions / they can be reminded of their childhood and of popular childhood stories / the films have wisdom in their simplicity.

❷ Elicit why it is important to look at the main areas covered in the notes before listening (by noting the structure, students will follow the talk more easily and not get lost, i.e. they will recognise when the speaker is moving on to a new area and be able to go to those questions).

- Remind students that by looking at the questions actively, i.e. by looking for the type of information and words they need, they will be more ready for the answers when they start to listen than if they merely read through the questions beforehand.
- Remind them also that by following the names in the notes, they should be able to follow the talk more easily.

Suggested answers
1 the history of animation technology and facts about Pixar Animation Studios, including future plans
2 There are three levels of help: You can listen for a) the bold headings that indicate a change in topic; b) the names and other words in the left-hand column, which act as prompts; and c) the words around each gap that help you predict the type of answer.
3 1 plural noun, something to do with faces
2 noun, a material used to make cut-outs for producing animated scenes
3 adjective, describes slides
4 a number, an amount of money
5 noun, a new animation feature that was included in *Monsters, Inc.*
6 noun, an animation technique used in *Finding Nemo*
7 noun, something that needs to be believable on screen
8 noun, aspect of humans
9 noun (singular or plural), something produced by a different type of company
10 noun, a style of animation

❸ Play the recording once. Students should note their answers while listening.

- When they have finished listening, give them some time to check and complete their answers
- Remind them that they will gain a mark for each

correct answer, but they do not have marks subtracted for wrong answers, so it is a good idea to make an intelligent guess for any gaps they have not been able to complete.

- Tell them to check that they have kept within the word limit (two words and/or a number).

> **Answers**
> 1 drawings   2 paper
> 3 hand-painted / hand painted   4 6.3 billion
> 5 (animal) fur   6 digital lighting   7 crowds
> 8 facial movement   9 video games   10 reality

Extension idea Ask students to check their answers with a partner, then listen again for any information they are not sure about. They can also check their spelling in a dictionary where necessary.

❹ ❺ ***Alternative treatment*** If you want to spend less time on these exercises, just ask students to work in pairs and discuss the questions.

Vocabulary Adjective + noun collocations

❶ ***As a warmer*** Write on the board: *reputation, problem, discovery*

- Ask students to work in pairs and think of adjectives they can use with each noun, e.g. *excellent reputation*. (*Suggested answers:* considerable/excellent/fine/good/great/bad/poor/international/professional **reputation**; big/great/serious/complicated/difficult/complex/main/urgent/insoluble **problem**; amazing/big/exciting/important/significant/major/latest, recent/accidental **discovery**.)
- Tell students that using collocations correctly will raise their band score in the exam, as they result in more natural-sounding English.

> **Answers**
> 2 plentiful   3 irreplaceable   4 extensive
> 5 primary   6 sure   7 tall

Extension idea Ask students to check the meanings of words in their dictionaries where necessary.

- Ask them to work in pairs and discuss when they would use one of the correct words and when the other in each case, e.g. *considerable* is a little more formal than *large* in Question 1. (*Suggested answers:* **2** *outstanding* is more extreme than *excellent*; **3** *significant* and *noteworthy* have different meanings; **4/5** there are no significant differences between the alternatives.)

❷ **Answers**
> 1 expectations; high/great   2 central/main characters   3 outstanding feature   4 considerable/large number   5 significant/noteworthy achievement

Extension idea Ask students to work in pairs and answer this question:
Why do you think electronic computer games are continuing to grow in popularity?

- Encourage them to use the collections from Exercise 1 and tell them to think for a few moments before they speak and to give fairly long answers (i.e. not just one sentence).

Speaking Parts 2 and 3

❶ ***As a warmer*** Ask students in small groups: *What things do you use the Internet for?*

- To replicate exam conditions, give students one minute to make notes.

❷ **Answers**

1	introduces her topic	✓ *The website I'm going to talk about is …*
2	introduces each point clearly	✓ *What it is is, it's basically a site where … What people do is … It's mainly young people who … I love this website because …*
3	paraphrases when she can't remember a word or phrase	✓ *… where you can listen to ordinary people, I mean people who aren't famous …*
4	repeats some points	✗
5	rephrases to avoid hesitation	✓ *… there are all sorts of … many different types of …*
6	uses a strategy to include something she forgot	✓ *I meant to say earlier …*
7	pauses unnecessarily	✗
8	ends her talk naturally within two minutes	✓ *… it's always really good.*

Extension idea Elicit why items 1, 2, 4 and 6 are good things to do in the test. (*Answers:* 1 and 2: clearly outlining and structuring your talk makes you easier to follow, shows you are covering the points in the task and are in control of the situation; 4 is a repair strategy which allowed Rosy to include an idea which had slipped out of the main structure of the talk; 6 shows ability to speak at length, keep going and that you have plenty of ideas to express.)

- Ask students to suggest other phrases they could use for 1, 2 and 4. (*Suggested answers:* **1** My favourite website is / The website I visit most often is; **2** The website consists of, Most people use it as/for, More than anything, it's a website for, I really enjoy the website because, I think the site is fantastic because; **4** Oh, and something I forgot to mention earlier.)

❸ *Alternative treatment* With books closed, ask students: *What can you do in the Speaking test when there's something you want to say, but you don't know the word?* Students should suggest some or all of the strategies a–d in the exercise.
- Tell students that using these strategies will create a positive impression, as they show the candidate has survival techniques and can paraphrase an unknown or forgotten word or phrase. Credit is given in the test for being able to do this, and it is expected of high-level candidates.

Answers
1 a and c: *ordinary people, I mean people who aren't famous, you know, not professionals*
2 c: *many different types of music*

❹ **Suggested answers**
1 in a special place – a building with rooms to record – where other people can record you
2 It sometimes looks like a huge table with a lot of buttons and switches, and there are microphones and amplifiers, too.
3 You can be any age.
4 people who write their own songs
5 someone who looks for talented people; notice
6 music that no one has heard before

Extension idea Read out the suggested answers above one by one and ask students which strategy (a–d) from Exercise 3 each is (*answers:* **1** c, **2** d, **3** c, **4** c, **5** c, **6** a).

❺ *Alternative treatment 1* Before they start, ask students to think of two or three things they can mention which they do not know the word for in English. Ask them to think of strategies for explaining these things and to include them in their talk.
- *Alternative treatment 2* Ask students to refer back to the four useful items in Exercise 2 before they start. While they are listening to their partner speaking, they should use these items as a checklist and give feedback afterwards.

❻ 🎧 *Alternative treatment* Before students listen, ask them to think of one point for and one point against each of the ideas expressed in the questions.

Answers
A 3   B 1   C 2

❼ Ask students to copy the phrases they have underlined into their notebooks for reference.

Answers
Katalina: a significant advantage for anyone is / Another is
Obi: there aren't many benefits to doing that
Elicia: one of the main drawbacks of using / A real benefit to children of using

❽ **Answers**
1 of   2 from   3 to   4 For   5 over

Extension idea Ask students to work in pairs and write four sentences about the advantages and disadvantages of mobile phones, using some of the phrases from this exercise and Exercise 7. You could also draw their attention to page 116 of the Language reference.

Note: this is a good time to do the Pronunciation section.

❾ *Alternative treatment* Divide the class into 'examiners' and 'candidates'. Ask examiners and candidates to work in together in pairs.
- Tell the examiners to ask each question in turn and to listen carefully to the answers; they should decide how well the candidate answered each question, what things they said which would give them a high band score, and things they said/ did not say which would give them a lower band score.
- When they have finished, they should give their partners feedback.
- They then change roles and do the exercise again.

Pronunciation Intonation 2

❶ 🎧 Point out that, in English, a monotone with little intonation or movement of the voice often denotes lack of interest, lack of engagement or even hostility.

Answers
1 Speaker a) sounds more interested; the tone rises on *not really* and *convenient*.
2 Speaker b) sounds bored; the tone is flat.

Extension idea Ask students to repeat sentence a) imitating the intonation.

❷ 🎧 Remind students that the voice moves most on the stressed syllables, so deciding where to place stress in a sentence will help with intonation, too.

Answers
1 right / yeah / agree / that
2 actually / I think / positive / one

❸ Tell students that there are a range of correct intonations involving movement of the voice to show interest, and that their answers may be possible even if they do not replicate the speakers completely.

- A good starting point is to identify the stress in the sentences.

Answers

a Oh, completely. There are CCTV cameras everywhere.

b I don't think people notice really – they're just used to it.

c I would, yes. Everywhere you go, there are screens of one kind or another.

d Well, you can't stop it – new developments are happening all the time.

e I'm not sure. In some ways it's a nuisance, but in others it isn't.

❹ ∩ Once students have listened, have them work in pairs to listen and repeat. See how much they can do from memory.

Writing Task 2

❶ *As a warmer* With books closed and students in small groups, ask: *How has IT improved people's lives? Are there any aspects which have got worse?*

- Tell students that they should brainstorm four or five benefits and four or five drawbacks. When they come to plan and write, they need not use them all.
- *Alternative treatment* Elicit what students should do first when they read a writing task (analyse the question, underlining the key ideas). Ask them to do this. (*Suggested underlining:* Information technology / dominates / home / leisure / work / To what extent / benefits outweigh the disadvantages)

Extension idea Ask students to use their lists to write a plan for their essay. When they have finished, they can compare their plan with those of other students.

❷ *Alternative treatment* If students did the extension idea in Exercise 1, ask them to compare their plan with the contents of the sample answer.

– *Which ideas are the same, and which are different?*
– *Which ideas in the sample answer do they think are particularly good?*

Answers
1 There are benefits and drawbacks, but the benefits are greater.

2 There are two paragraphs on drawbacks, followed by two on benefits. The writer places the benefits last, and uses this to lead into the conclusion.

3 Yes: home, work and leisure are all mentioned.

4 Using a discourse marker that clearly shows a link between the two drawbacks: *A related criticism …*

5 Using a discourse marker that shows he is going to discuss the other side of the argument: *Despite these drawbacks …*

6 Using a simple linker (*also*) to show that he is going to add more benefits to those in paragraph 4.

7 It concedes that there are drawbacks; it re-states the writer's view; it draws together points related to home, work and leisure.

❸ Tell students that using discourse markers helps readers to follow the argument clearly and will help them to achieve a higher band score in the exam.

Answers
1 Having said that …
2 while
3 although, whereas, in spite of this, however, nevertheless, even though, on the other hand

❹ **Answers**
2 detrimental   3 biggest   4 regular
5 access   6 huge   7 invaluable

Extension idea Ask students to work in pairs and decide what each of the collocations means, looking at the context in the sample answer.

- They can then check their answers in dictionaries.
- Tell them to copy the phrases into their notebooks and refer to them before they do the writing task (*answers:* an integral part = necessary or important as part of; a detrimental effect = a harmful or damaging effect; biggest drawbacks = greatest disadvantages; take regular exercise = take exercise repeatedly in a fixed pattern; instant access = ability to reach or obtain something immediately; huge benefits = great advantages; an invaluable resource = an extremely useful tool).

❺ **Answers**
1 detrimental effect   2 huge benefits   3 invaluable resource   4 integral part   5 biggest drawbacks; instant access   6 take regular exercise

Extension idea Ask students to work alone and choose four of the collocations to write their own example sentences. They then work in small groups and read their sentences to each other.

Note: this would be a good time to look at the Key grammar section.

6 *Extension idea* When they have finished, ask students to compare their plans with another pair of students. They can then make any adjustments to their plan that they wish to before writing.

7 This exercise is probably best done at home. However, for exam practice, tell students that they should aim to complete the task in 40 minutes, including reading through and checking their answer afterwards.

Sample answer

Mobile technology has become an integral part of our lives, and the existence of mobile phones, laptops and iPads has altered the way many people work. While there are distinct advantages to this, it is important to guard against over use and possible detrimental effects on health and relationships.

One of the biggest benefits of mobile technology is that people no longer have to work in an office. In fact, many businesses now permit their staff to work from home on some days of the week. This is particularly helpful for busy parents; it can reduce stress levels and help people manage their daily lives better.

Another benefit for many people and businesses is that work can continue outside the office. Phone calls can be made almost anywhere, and documents can be read or written on public transport or in cafés. This is extremely beneficial for people who have long trips to work.

Despite the advantages mentioned above, care must be taken to ensure that the convenience of 'teleworking' does not lead to more hours on the job and less time spent doing exercise or being with friends and family. No one would deny that it is wonderful to be able to work from home, but a person who spends too much time on their computer may find that their health suffers in the long run.

Similarly, anyone who enjoys the benefits of working on public transport needs to make sure that they consider other people around them. In my city, there are notices that warn travellers not to talk loudly on their phones; in others, there are mobile-free carriages on trains because companies have had so many complaints.

On the whole, most people profit from the use of mobile technology, and there are obvious advantages to its use. However, we need to keep an eye on how much we rely on this resource, otherwise the disadvantages will be greater for everyone.

Key grammar Referencing

1 Students have already worked on referencing in the Reading section, Exercise 4.
- Elicit why referencing is important (*answers:* to make your writing more coherent and easy to follow; to avoid repetition of vocabulary items and so reduce the number of words used).
- *Alternative treatment* Ask students to look back to Exercise 4 in the Reading section and note what sort of words are used for referencing before they do this exercise.

Answers
1 that   2 these   3 it   4 their

---

2 Point out to students how the use of these references makes the writing more economical – fewer words are necessary to express the idea.

Answers
1 the time spent reading emails and chatting online
2 not going out or taking regular exercise
3 800 million active users

---

3 Tell students that they need to be particularly careful with singular and plural agreement of *it/they, this/these* and *that/those.*
- Point out that mistakes using reference devices can lead to considerable misunderstanding.

Answers
3 ~~for~~ for it   4 ~~this two~~ these two   5 ~~such~~ this
6 ~~it~~ them   7 ~~Other~~ Another

---

4 **Answers**
1 this/that   2 they   3 these/such
4 one/them   5 that   6 it/this

Vocabulary and grammar review

Unit 5

Answers
1 **2** whilst **3** first **4** Once **5** next **6** Following that
   7 Meanwhile **8** eventually
2 **2** irreversible **3** overcrowded **4** meaningless
   5 misunderstood **6** impatient **7** unnecessary
3 **2** wouldn't have included **3** I'd **4** might have been
   5 I'd never have become **6** might **7** had had
4 **2** ... put up, encouraging walkers to take another
      route.
   3 ... well camouflaged, enabling them to take their
      prey by surprise.
   4 ... deep waters, making it hard for divers to locate
      the wreck.
   5 ... capsized ship, resulting in a treacherous zone
      for marine life.

Unit 6

Answers
1 **2** innovative/convincing/outstanding **3** first
   4 high **5** outstanding/innovative
   6 able/outstanding **7** convincing **8** private
2 **2** to/in/of **3** of **4** from **5** for **6** over **7** to
3 **2** ~~such~~ this/that **3** ~~it~~ they **4** ~~the other~~ another
   5 ~~ones~~ others **6** ~~neither~~ none **7** ~~it~~ so/this
   8 ~~them~~ it
4 **2** this figure **3** this technique **4** that success
   5 other factors **6** this type of problem

Unit 6 photocopiable activity
Talk around IT!

Time: 40 minutes

Objectives
- To practise using different strategies for when you don't know a word
- To revise and practise the correct use of prepositions when talking about advantages and disadvantages
- To revise adjective–noun collocations
- To raise awareness of intonation for showing interest
- To expand and consolidate vocabulary related to IT

Before class

Make a photocopy of the worksheet on page 84 and cut it up so that each group of students has one set of grey and one set of white cards. You can also make a copy of the Rules at the end of these notes for each group of three/four students.

❶ As a warmer Elicit at least four strategies which can be used when you don't know a word (see Unit 6 of the Student's Book) and write these on the board. They could include:
- saying what something is not
- explaining how something works
- giving a definition
- describing what something looks like
- giving an example.

❷ Tell students that they are going to play a speaking game which will help them to practise these strategies. Ask them to work in groups of three or four and place both sets of cards (grey and white) in two separate piles, face down, in the middle of each group. Show the class how to play the game by demonstrating a typical turn of each type.

First, take a 'Talk around IT' card and talk for about one minute, using as many of the strategies from the Warmer activity as possible. After you have finished, ask students if they can guess the word you were trying to talk around. Remind them that, during the game, they have to wait until the end of their opponent's speech before making their guess. Then demonstrate the 'Correction challenge' by asking a student to pick up a card and read the sentence aloud to you. Say whether it is correct or not, giving the correct version where appropriate. Explain that the errors on the cards are all related to prepositions and collocations. Deal with any questions from students about how to play.

Alternative treatment With a weaker group, ask students to work in pairs (two or three pairs in each group). Instead of being placed face down in the middle, the grey cards are distributed equally before the game starts. There is then a 'conferring' phase when the pairs can check they know the meaning of all their grey-card items, or prepare their guesses, before play begins. When it is a pair's turn, they can either use a grey card of their choice, or respond to a white challenge card from the table.

❸ Before starting, explain to students that, during the game, they should listen carefully to the other group members and count the number of different strategies they use in each turn. A player who manages to use at least four strategies in a single turn can keep the card regardless of whether the other students can guess the word at the end.

❹ When all the groups have finished playing, ask each group to report back on how well they managed with the strategies. Ask: *Which one would you find most useful for the IELTS Speaking test?*

- - - - - - - - - - - - - - ✂ - - - - - - - - - - - -

Rules
- Take turns to play the game. When it is a player's turn, he/she should choose a 'Talk around IT' or 'Correction Challenge' card.
- For 'Talk around IT', the player whose turn it is must pick up a white card, without showing it to the others, and talk for one or two minutes without mentioning any of the words on the card. When the time is up, if the other students are able to guess which word is on the card, the speaker may keep the card. If not, he/she must put the card to one side on the waste pile. If the other students are not able to guess the word, or if the speaker mentions the word by accident, their turn does not count and they must throw away their card. However, if a player manages to use four or more strategies during their turn, they can keep the card regardless of whether the others can guess the word.
- For 'Correction challenge' cards, the sentence in *italics* (not the answer) is read out by another player. The player whose turn it is must say whether the sentence contains any errors with collocations or prepositions. If the sentence is not correct, the player must correct it. The reader then reveals the right answer. If the player has got the answer right, he/she may keep the card. If not, he/she must put the card to one side on the waste pile.
- Play then passes to the left until all the cards have been used up, or until a time limit has been reached. The winner of the game is the player who manages to keep the most cards.

Unit 6 photocopiable activity
Talk around IT!

'Talk around IT' cards

an animated film	social-networking websites	download speed	an MP3 player
anti-virus software	a hacker	CCTV cameras	a search engine
a wireless internet connection	Wikipedia	a satellite navigation system	teleworking
a tablet computer	an online bank account	chatting online	a mouse
a mobile phone app	a webcam	a memory stick	a laptop computer

'Correction challenge' cards

People of all ages can benefit with using the Internet. (✗ People of all ages can benefit **from** using the Internet.)	*The government should provide everyone with free access to the Internet.* (✔ This sentence is correct.)
Smartphones have a number of advantages over the devices which were previously available. (✔ This sentence is correct.)	*Mobile phones have a number of benefits to both parents and children.* (✗ Mobile phones have a number of benefits **for** both parents and children.)
One of the advantages for shopping online is that you don't need to leave your home. (✗ One of the advantages **of** shopping online is that you don't need to leave your home.)	*This negative view of the Internet is not based in reliable evidence.* (✗ This negative view of the Internet is not based **on** reliable evidence.)
There are a number of drawbacks from this kind of technology. (✗ There are a number of drawbacks **to** this kind of technology.)	*Online shopping is growing in popularity.* (✔ This sentence is correct.)
There are positive and negative aspects to internet banking. (✔ This sentence is correct.)	*It's important not to become dependent from information technology.* (✗ It's important not to become dependent **on** information technology.)
Some parents are critical to social networking sites. (✗ Some parents are critical **of** social networking sites.)	*We need to ask ourselves what the benefits from this kind of technology are.* (✗ We need to ask ourselves what the benefits **of** this kind of technology are.)
The Internet has had a positive effect to economic development. (✗ The Internet has had a positive effect **on** economic development.)	*Nowadays, many people prefer to download music directly from the Internet.* (✔ This sentence is correct.)
A huge amount of useful information is available in the Internet. (✗ A huge amount of useful information is available **on** the Internet.)	*You can register on the website by following the in-screen instructions.* (✗ You can register on the website by following the **on**-screen instructions.)

Word list

Unit 6

the advent of something *phrase* (RS) the start or arrival of something new

advocate of something *np* [C] (64) someone who supports a particular idea or way of doing things

anything but (sophisticated) *phrase* (63) If someone or something is anything but a particular quality, they are the opposite of that quality.

break new ground *phrase* (RS) to do something that is different from anything that has been done before

by and large *phrase* (64) generally

cater to someone/something *vp* [T] (64) to give people what they want, usually something that people think is wrong

convincing *adj* (RS) able to make you believe that something is true or right

enamoured with someone/something *adj* (64) liking or approving of someone or something very much

engage in something *vp* [T] (69) to take part in something

the extent of something *phrase* (65) the level, size or importance of something

feature film *np* [C] (RS) a film that is usually 90 or more minutes long

film sequence *np* [C] (RS) a part of a film that deals with one event

generate *v* [T] (63) to cause something to exist

get stuck *phrase* (63) to not be able to continue doing something because there is something you cannot understand or solve

gloss over something *vp* [T] (64) to avoid discussing something, or to discuss something without any details in order to make it seem unimportant

icon *n* [C] (RS) a person or thing that is famous because it represents a particular idea or way of life

identify with someone *vp* [T] (68) to feel that you are similar to someone, and can understand them or their situation because of this

in essence *phrase* (64) relating to the most important characteristics or ideas of something

in leaps and bounds *phrase* (70) If progress or growth happens in leaps and bounds, it happens very quickly.

in vain *phrase* (63) without any success

instant access *np* [U] (70) the opportunity to use or see something immediately

mediocrity *n* [U] (64) the quality of being not very good

modify *v* [T] (64) to change something in order to improve it

overhaul *v* [T] (63) to make important changes to a system in order to improve it

pace *singular n* (63) the speed at which something happens

phenomena *plural n* (RS) things that exist or happen, usually things that are unusual

pioneer *v* [T] (RS) to be one of the first people to do something

prove to be something *v* (71) to show a particular quality after a period of time

reach the point *phrase* (70) to get to a particular situation

require someone to do something *v* [T] (66) to need someone to do something

rote *n* (64) a way of learning something by repeating it many times, rather than understanding it

save the day *phrase* (63) to do something that solves a serious problem

scroll up/down/back/forward, etc. *v* [I] (63) to move text or an image on a computer screen so that you can look at the part that you want

simulation *n* [C/U] (67) when you do or make something which behaves or looks like something real but which is not real

supplement *v* [T] (66) to add an extra amount or part to something

supplement *n* [C] (63) an extra amount or part added to something

tailor *v* [T] (63) to make or change something so that it is suitable

technique *n* [C/U] (64) a particular or special way of doing something

tune out *vp* [I] (63) to stop giving your attention to what is happening around you

unambiguously *adv* (64) clearly having only one meaning

Vocabulary extension

Unit 6

adopt a system or approach *vp* [T] to start using a particular system or way of dealing with something

blog *n* [C] a record of your thoughts that you put on the Internet for other people to read

browse the web *vp* [T] to look at information on the Internet

cartoon strip *np* [C] several funny drawings showing the same character or characters doing different things

caricature *n* [C] a funny drawing or description of someone, especially someone famous, which makes part of their appearance or character more noticeable than it really is

computer literate *adj* able to use a computer

couch-potato *n* [C] (informal) a lazy person who spends too much time watching television

creature of habit *np* [C] a person who always does the same thing in the same way

electronic gadget *np* [C] a small piece of equipment that does a particular job and uses electricity

embrace change *vp* [T] to accept new ideas, beliefs, methods, etc. in an enthusiastic way

feature *v* [T] to include someone or something as an important part

hard copy *np* [C/U] information from a computer that has been printed on paper

hectic *adj* extremely busy and full of activity

globalisation *n* [U] the increase of business around the world, especially by big companies operating in many countries

implement a project *vp* [T] to make a project start to happen

infrastructure *n* [C] the basic systems, such as transport and communication, that a country or organisation uses in order to work effectively

interactive *adj* Interactive computer programs, games, etc. react to the way that you use them.

nanotechnology *n* [U] an area of science which deals with developing and producing extremely small tools and machines by controlling the arrangement of separate atoms

navigate a site *vp* [T] to successfully find information and perform functions on a website

online *adj, adv* connected to a system of computers, especially the Internet

outsource a project/work *vp* [T] If a company outsources a project or work, it pays to have that project or that work done by another company.

portable *adj* small and light enough to be carried / able to be used in different situations

resource *n* [C] something that a country, person or organisation has which they can use

secure site *np* [C] a website in which the information sent from that site by a particular user cannot be accessed by anyone else

sedentary lifestyle *np* [C] a way of living that involves spending a lot of time sitting down and very little time being active

specialise in something *vp* [T] to know a lot about a particular subject, usually a subject that is your work

state-of-the-art *adj* using the newest ideas, technology and materials

telecommunications *n* [U] the process or business of sending information or messages by telephone, radio, etc.

upgrade *v* [T] to improve something so that it is of a higher quality or a newer version

upgrade *n* [C] a newer or improved version of something

virtual *adj* using computer images and sounds that make you think an imagined situation is real

web-based *adj* Web-based software is software that you can use over the Internet using a browser (= a program which lets you look at pages on the Internet).

with one click *phrase* If you can do something on a computer, phone, etc. with one click, you can do it by clicking a mouse or by pressing a button.

❶ Match a verb from Box A with the rest of the phrase or idiom from Box B. Then complete the sentences below with the full phrase or idiom in the appropriate form.

A	break	~~catch~~	keep	maintain	B	links with	new ground	the clock back	the day
	reach	save	turn			the point where	themselves to themselves		~~up on~~

0 Having not done any recent reading or research into this topic, I feel I have a lot to
...catch..up..on.... .

1 The department has always .... with the British Museum and regularly arranges student visits there.

2 Having spent such a long time working on this research project, I have .... I have lost interest in it.

3 It seemed as though the project would fail due to lack of funding, but fortunately a private donor came forward at the last minute and ....

4 It would be very interesting to .... to be able to really understand how people used to live.

5 My work colleagues are very pleasant, but they generally .... and don't socialise.

6 This exciting research has .... in the field of anthropology.

❷ Complete these sentences with the correct form of the words in brackets.

0 The fire at the museum led to the destruction of many exhibits, most of which are
...irreplaceable.... . *(replace)*

1 Before its eventual fall, the Roman empire became increasingly .... *(stable)*

2 They totally .... the amount of time and money the project would require. *(estimate)*

3 The expedition covered thousands of miles and ventured into difficult and .... terrain. *(hospitable)*

4 Industrial growth in Britain was rapid in the first half of the 1800s, but started to .... towards the end of the century. *(accelerate)*

5 His argument didn't make sense and was totally .... *(logical)*

6 Unfortunately, although these old paintings look valuable, they are completely .... *(worth)*

❸ Complete these sentences by writing the correct preposition (*by, for, with, to*, etc.) in each gap.

0 One drawback ....of..... the widespread use of mobile phones is a decline in language skills amongst young people.

1 The introduction of the new software will have several benefits .... our company.

2 This proposal has many advantages .... the previous one.

3 One disadvantage .... young people using the Internet is the large number of unsuitable websites.

4 Although the introduction of a new computer system was very costly, few of the workers felt they gained much benefit .... it.

5 Have a look at this website; it might be of benefit .... you.

④ Complete each of the adjective + noun collocations in the sentences below using a suitable adjective from the box.

detrimental	~~high~~	huge	instant	integral	large	noteworthy

0 She had ....*high*........ expectations about the launch of her latest feature film.

1 One of the most .... achievements of the twentieth century must be the creation of the World Wide Web.

2 Many people believe the use of mobile phones for texting has had a .... effect on language skills.

3 Broadband technology has brought .... benefits to many companies.

4 This new app gives you .... access to over a million free books on the Internet.

5 A .... number of products have been returned due to their substandard quality.

6 Technology is an .... part of modern-day education.

⑤ Choose the best option in italics to complete each of these sentences.

0 If I'd known how significant the discovery was, I *would take / (would have taken)* more interest in it.

1 Were it not for the work of archaeologists, we *wouldn't have / didn't have* such a good understanding of ancient civilisations.

2 We *would never have found / would never find* the buried remains if we hadn't got lost.

3 If I *didn't have / wouldn't have* a degree in history, I'd never have got the job.

4 I wouldn't visit a museum *unless / on condition* that you paid me – I hate them!

5 If I *hadn't seen / didn't see* the evidence with my own eyes, I wouldn't know the truth now.

6 *Did we have / Had we had* more funding, we would have been able to continue our research.

⑥ Complete these sentences by writing a suitable reference word in each gap.

0 Thirty years ago, only a few families owned two or more cars; nowadays ....*such*........ households are very common.

1 I find it quite difficult to navigate .... type of website.

2 I tried to download the documents, but I had great difficulty doing ....

3 The price of new items of technology tends to be quite high when they first appear. .... does not stop many people from buying the item immediately.

4 Mobile phones are so much a part of people's lives that many would find it difficult to live without ....

5 There were two suitable laptops in my price range, but unfortunately .... of them was in stock.

6 The fall in sales has led to a number of store closures across the country. .... has also resulted in the launch of a new marketing campaign.

7 Rewrite each sentence or pair of sentences, using a participle clause to express the consequence.

0   The cliff was slowly eroded by waves. This meant that fossils in the buried rock eventually became visible.

The cliff was slowly eroded by waves, meaning that fossils in the buried rock eventually became visible.

1   Two thousand years ago, the Romans invaded large parts of the world. This influenced many aspects of life.

....

....

2   The writing in some of these documents is very unclear, which makes it difficult to read.

....

....

3   Even in ancient times, Homo sapiens travelled great distances. This enabled them to buy, sell and exchange useful materials.

....

....

4   During the medieval period, many castles were built, which protected the land from enemies.

....

....

5   The ancient Greeks influenced many areas of life. These include science, politics, philosophy and the arts.

....

....

Unit 7 Our relationship with nature

Unit objectives

- **Listening Section 3:** thinking about synonyms and paraphrasing; sentence completion; identifying locations; labelling a plan; short-answer questions
- **Vocabulary:** idiomatic expressions
- **Reading Section 2:** skimming; time management in the test; matching headings; sentence completion; pick from a list
- **Speaking Parts 2 and 3:** using linking words and phrases; using more advanced vocabulary; speculating and talking about the future
- **Pronunciation:** word stress
- **Key grammar:** speculating and talking about the future
- **Writing Task 1:** working with information from two or more sources; planning; paragraphing; using commas correctly; using synonyms to avoid repetition

Starting off

❶ *As a warmer* Ask students to work in pairs and discuss: *In what ways are animals important in our lives? (Suggested answers:* for food, for clothing, as company, as transport, as part of our environment, as part of our ecosystem, for entertainment, etc.)

- *Background note* Sometimes a subheading may contain words or expressions that are unfamiliar to students or that are not being used in their literal sense. For example, in subheading E, *What's black and white and adored all over* relates to an old English riddle (Q: What's black and white and red all over? A: A newspaper (read all over)) However, the meaning can be worked out without knowing the riddle. In the live exam, subheadings will always be written in a way which is reasonably transparent to candidates.
- *Alternative treatment* Ask students to underline unfamiliar vocabulary in the subheadings. When they have matched the subheadings with the photos, ask them to guess possible meanings for the vocabulary from the relationship between the subheading and the photo.

Answers
1 C 2 D 3 A 4 B 5 E

❷ Encourage students to discuss and give reasons for their choices.

Answers
1 B 2 A 3 C 4 E 5 D

❸ *Alternative treatment* Before looking at the original titles on page 96, round up ideas from the whole class and ask them to vote for the best title for each article, which you write on the board. They then compare these best titles with the originals and say which they think is better, and why.

❹ *As a warmer* Ask students if they ever read articles about wildlife, or watch wildlife documentaries on TV. Why? / Why not?

- Tell students that animals/wildlife is a frequent topic area in IELTS tests and that reading articles of this type will help to prepare them.

Listening Section 3

❶ *As a warmer* Ask students to look at the photos in Starting off again and say which photo they find the most interesting or most beautiful. Which photo is the best encouragement to read the article?

- *Alternative treatment* When students answer the first two questions, ask them to use the photos from Starting off to support their ideas.

Suggested answers
1 Animals are less predictable than people / Scenery needs to have a focus to make it interesting
2 colour and light / balanced features / animals behaving in an interesting manner

❷ Labelling a plan tests students' ability to understand language describing locations and directions, and listen for specific information or details.

Tell students that it is important to study the plan or map before they listen to see where things are located in relation to each owther, because this is what the recording will focus on when they listen.

- *Alternative treatment* If you think your students need it, revise language for describing location and giving directions:
  - tell them that sometimes maps and plans will have compass directions on them and they will hear compass directions. Point them to the compass directions on the plan.
  - ask them for synonyms of *next to* (*answers:* beside, by). Ask: *Where is B on the plan?* (*Answer:* next to / beside / by Loch Affric)
  - write these words/phrases on the board and check students know the meaning of each: *next to, beside, opposite, in front of, across, on the other side of, beyond, behind, near, between, among, over.*

> **Suggested answers**
> 1 an area of Scotland with lochs (lakes), wooded and non-wooded ground
> 2 five areas: largest in the south-east / three smaller areas either side of the lochs and where the lochs meet / smallest area on the south shore of one of the lochs
> 3 The lochs are long and thin and run across the map from south-west to north-east.
> 4 three; all in the non-wooded areas – two in the south and one in the north

Extension idea Bring maps or plans from your local tourist office to class.
- Ask students to work in small groups and take turns to describe where things are on the maps. The other students in the group should say what thing or place the speaker is describing.

❸

> Short-answer questions tend to test students' ability to understand factual information and especially their ability to distinguish between main ideas and details.

Remind students that:
- they may have to deal with more than one type of task in each part of the listening (here, labelling a plan and short-answer questions)
- they need to check the instructions carefully to see how many words and/or numbers they should write.

> **Suggested underlining**
> 4 What / cause / miss / photograph
> 5 quality / photographers / need

❹ ∩ Play the recording once only.
- Give students time to complete their answers and compare them with their partners' answers.
- *Alternative treatment* Play the recording again for them to check their answers, but remind them they will hear the recording once only in the exam.

> **Answers**
> 1 C   2 F   3 A
> 4 hesitation/hesitating/waiting   5 patience

Extension ideas
1 Ask students to spell out the answers to Questions 4 and 5 while you or another student writes the answer on the board.
   - Remind students that answers must be spelled correctly in the exam.
2 Ask students to look at the three Exam advice boxes in this section and, in pairs, say which advice they think is the most useful.

❺

> Sentence-completion tasks test students' abilities to understand the main ideas in what they listen to and to relate these to gapped details in sentences.

Tell students that, in the exam, if they can think of paraphrases for the key ideas while they are underlining, this will help them to focus on how the ideas might be expressed, but that the main priority is to decide what information they need for each gap and thus know what to listen for.
- Check that students have read the task instructions. Ask: *How many words can you write?* (*Answer:* one or two) *Will any of the answers be numbers?* (*Answer:* No)
- Remind students that they should always check completion-task instructions, as there will be some variation between them.
- When students have finished, round up their ideas for both questions with the whole class and discuss as necessary.

> **Suggested answers**
> 1 *Suggested underlining*
>   6 bad weather, think more carefully
>   7 Take advantage / near water
>   8 equipment / 'angle finder' / avoid
>   9 work / artists / ideas
>   10 Think about / issues / deciding
> 2 6 something affected by weather
>   7 something linked to water
>   8 something helped by an angle finder
>   9 people who help produce ideas
>   10 issues that affect a photo

❻ Tell students they should note down their answers as they listen, but they will have a short time at the end to complete them.

- 🎧 Play the recording once only, then give students time to complete their answers.
- Tell them that they should make intelligent guesses where they did not hear the exact words.
- When students have finished, ask them to compare their answers in pairs. Then play the recording again for them to check.

> **Answers**
> 6 landscape   7 (a/the) reflection(s)
> 8 (neck) pain   9 designers   10 conservation

Extension idea

Ask students: *What paraphrases were used to express the key ideas in the questions?* (*Answers:* think more carefully – take ... into account; take advantage of – make the most of; avoid – prevent; work of artists – wildlife paintings by Scottish artists; generate ideas – help me get ideas; Think about ... issues – consider matters related to ...) Students should work in pairs and answer from memory.

- When they have finished, play the recording again for them to check.

❼ Students should recognise that this task is similar to Speaking Part 2. Remind them to note down particular vocabulary they want to use.

- When they speak, remind them to introduce, structure and round off their talks.

Extension idea Ask students:

- *What do you particularly like taking photos of?*
- *What, for you, are the most interesting photos?*
- *What elements make a photo interesting to look at?*

Vocabulary Idiomatic expressions

❶ *As a warmer* With books closed, write on the board: *We like to put new people in the picture as soon as they arrive.* Ask: *What do you think* put someone in the picture *means?* (*Answer:* to inform someone about a situation)

- Ask students to work in small groups and think of other idiomatic expressions they know.
- Round up with the whole class, writing useful expressions on the board and asking students to explain what they mean.
- With books open, ask students to do the exercise. When they have finished, they can check their answers in the recording script on page 158.

> **Answers**
> 1 experience   2 breath   3 run   4 account
> 5 most   6 time   7 bear

Extension idea Ask students to underline the expressions in the recording script on page 158 and, in pairs, to discuss what each of them means in the context without looking at Exercise 2 in the unit.

- When they have finished, they can check their ideas by looking at Exercise 2.

❷ **Answers**
> 1 make the most of   2 put it down to experience
> 3 take your time   4 in the long run
> 5 take your breath away
> 6 take into account; bear in mind

Extension idea Ask students to write their own sentences using these expressions.

- When they have finished, ask students to read out some of their sentences to the whole class, who say if the expressions have been used correctly and naturally.

❸ Tell, or elicit from, students that *turn out* in item 6 means 'have a particular result, especially an unexpected one' (*CALD*).

- *Alternative treatment* Ask students to work alone and think of a time when they did or felt each of these things.
- They then work in pairs and tell their partner about each of these occasions.

Reading Section 2

❶ *As a warmer* With books closed, ask students:

- *How long is the Reading paper?*
  (*Answer:* one hour)
- *How many sections does it contain?*
  (*Answer:* three)
- *How do you think you should manage your time in the Reading paper?*
- This last question might give rise to some discussion, especially as the sections get harder as the paper progresses. However, as in most exams, time management is an essential issue. It may be useful if the following points arise:
  - Students should spend a maximum of 20 minutes per section. If they spend longer on one section, they will have less time for a later, more difficult section and seriously limit their chances of achieving a high band score.

- They should skim the passage in two or three minutes before tackling the Reading tasks. Experience of doing the Reading sections in this course will have told them that many of the tasks require them to scan to find the right part of the passage to answer the question, something a preliminary skim will help them with.
- They should manage their time within each section, so that if they know they have 18 minutes (after skimming) and 13 questions, they should be spending about one and a half minutes on each question. So if a section has, say, six questions, it should take students about nine minutes to complete.

- With books open, students should do the exercise. When they have finished, discuss their answers as a whole-class activity and explain the comments in the answers below.

Answers
1 *in which they come* (The passages are graded in terms of difficulty.)
2 *a maximum of* (You only have an hour to do the test. Time management is an important part of any exam, and keeping a strict control on each section means that you will have the full 20 minutes you will need for the final, most difficult section.)
3 *Do the tasks in the order they occur.* (Work through things steadily and systematically. You should deal with each question while the passage is fresh in your mind. You probably won't have time to come back to certain questions later. You should have a strategy for each task type. The questions vary in difficulty, so even if you don't like a task type, the questions in it may not be as hard as you think.)
4 *need not* (Only completion tasks need to be written in full. Letters and 'T', 'F', 'NG' or 'Y', 'N', 'NG' are acceptable for other tasks. Writing answers in full when it is not necessary wastes time.)
5 *guess the answer* (Even if you're not sure of an answer, guess and write something. You might be right.)
6 *must* (Incorrect spellings are marked wrong.)

Extension idea Ask students to work in pairs and write two more pieces of advice on how to do the Reading paper.

- They then read these out to the whole class, who discuss how good the advice is.

❷ Even if you did *As a warmer* in Exercise 1, elicit why skimming is important (*answer*: for students to familiarise themselves with the contents and structure of the passage so that they can locate information more quickly when they do the tasks).

- Elicit from students that they should also check the title and subheading (which they have already seen in Starting off).
- When they skim, be strict with the time limit. With a good class, set the time limit at two minutes.
- ***Alternative treatment*** Remind students that, in the live exam, they will not have a multiple-choice skimming task. Ask them to skim the passage and then, with a partner, briefly say what it is about.

Answers
1 c (a and b are mentioned, but are not the main idea)
2 *Suggested answers*
   Matching headings: 10 minutes
   Sentence completion: 4 minutes
   Pick from a list: 4 minutes

---

❸ Remind students they did this task in Unit 2 on page 19.
- Refer them back to the Exam advice box on page 19.
- Elicit that the best way to do this task is to:
  - underline the key ideas in the list of headings first, so that students are familiar with the headings before they start reading
  - read the sections and answer the questions one by one, identifying the main idea in the section and then matching it to a heading.
- Where they are not sure which heading to choose for a particular section, they should make a note in pencil of the headings they think are possible and come back to it when they have answered the other questions in the task.
- Remind students that sometimes they may underline the whole heading as a key idea. This does not matter: the important thing is that they are thinking about the meaning of each heading.

Suggested underlining
i   Looking / clues
ii   Blaming / beekeepers
iii Solutions / more troublesome issue
iv   new bee species
v   impossible task / human
vi   preferred pollinator
vii features / suit / pollinator
viii obvious / less obvious pollen carriers
ix   undesirable alternative
x   unexpected setback

Answers

1 v (*Growers have tried numerous ways to rattle pollen from tomato blossoms. They have used shaking tables, air blowers and blasts of sound.*)

2 viii (*What's astonishing is the array of workers that do it … Most surprising, some lizards …*)

3 vi (*Now at least a hundred commercial crops rely almost entirely on managed honeybees, which beekeepers raise and rent out to tend to big farms. And although other species of bees are five to ten times more efficient, on a per-bee basis, at pollinating certain fruits, honeybees have bigger colonies, cover longer distances, and tolerate management and movement better than most insects.*)

4 x (*… but in 2006 came an extreme blow … Beekeepers would lift the lid of a hive and be amazed to find only the queen and a few stragglers, the worker bees gone. In the US, a third to half of all hives crashed; some beekeepers reported colony losses near 90 percent. The mysterious culprit was named colony collapse disorder …*)

5 i (*When it first hit, many people, from agronomists to the public, assumed that our slathering of chemicals on agricultural fields was to blame for the mystery … It's hard to tease apart factors and outcomes, Pettis says … 'I only wish we had a single agent … that would make our work much easier.'*)

6 iii (*… habitat loss and alteration … are even more of a menace to pollinators than pathogens.*)

7 ix (*Take away that variety, and we'll lose more than honey. 'We wouldn't starve,' says Kremen. 'But what we eat, and even what we wear – pollinators, after all, give us some of our cotton and flax – would be limited to crops whose pollen travels by other means. 'In a sense,' she says, 'our lives would be dictated by the wind.'*)

Extension idea When students have finished, ask them to compare their answers in pairs, quoting from the passage to justify their choices.

❹ *Alternative treatment* Ask students to cover the instructions for this exercise and just look at the task.

- Remind them that they did this type of task in Unit 5 (when reading about early humans). Ask students to work in pairs and decide what the best procedure is for dealing with this task.
- When they have finished, they can uncover the instructions and compare them with their ideas.

- If necessary, discuss the procedure further, but remind students that there are a range of tasks in the Reading paper which require students to identify key ideas or key words before scanning the passage to find where they are mentioned, and that if they are going to cover all 40 Reading questions in one hour successfully, they need to adopt these techniques as routine.

Answers

1 *Suggested underlining*

   8 Both / first creatures / pollinate (two types of creature)

   9 Monkeys transport pollen (somewhere on a monkey's body)

   10 Honeybees / favoured / because / travel (an area)

   11 feature / CCD / loss (something in a bee hive affected by CCD)

2 8 flies and beetles 9 (furry) coats
   10 (longer) distances 11 worker bees

❺ Remind students that it is very easy to lose a mark through carelessness. Ask students which of the mistakes (a–e) they made.

- *Alternative treatment* Write the examples from the answers below on the board in random order. Ask students to say which mistake each is an example of.

Answers

a 8, 9, 10 and 11 (e.g. long distance) b 8, 9 and 11 (e.g. beetle, be) c 8 (e.g. flies not flies and beetles) d 10 (e.g. travel long distances) e 9, 11

❻ Tell students they practised this task in Unit 2 on page 21. Elicit the best procedure for dealing with this task.

- With 'pick from a list' and 'multiple-choice questions', they should read the question, then read the relevant part of the passage. Once they have understood the passage, they should read the options and choose the correct answer(s). If they read the options before reading the passage, they are more likely to be confused.

Suggested underlining
TWO methods / combating / CCD
Answers
12 C (*Claire Kremen encourages farmers … useful insects.* (paragraph F))
13 E (*It's vital that we … ease the burden on managed bees by letting native animals do their part …* (paragraph G))

❼ Ask students to treat these as Speaking Part 3 questions and to give fairly general (not personal) answers, supported by reasons and examples.

Speaking Parts 2 and 3

❶ *As a warmer* Write the names of five or six countries on the board (for example, China, Russia, Peru, Kenya and Australia, or the countries your students come from if it is a multinational class). Ask students in pairs: *What animals or plants do you associate with each of these countries?* (For the examples given, the animals could be China – pandas, Russia – bears, Peru – llamas, Kenya – any of many African animals, Australia – kangaroos or koalas.)

- *Alternative treatment* As students are now near the end of the course, ask them to work alone and take a minute to prepare and make notes.

❷ 🎧 When answering the second and third questions, elicit or point out that Daeng:
- does not deal with the points on the prompt card in order
- uses the phrases to either sum up a point she has been making, or introduce a point which she later supports with explanations and/or examples.
- As a result of using the phrases, she deals with the whole task in a coherent manner.

Answers
1 **b** very fond   **c** are everywhere   **d** are falling; publicity about   **e** important creatures
2 a) and e) focus on the importance of elephants and cover the opening and final points on the task.
b) relates to the second point (whether people like or dislike it).
c) relates to the first point (where you can find it).
d) relates to the third point (what recent news there has been about it).
3 They introduce or sum up her points.

❸ Remind students that they will be assessed on the range and appropriateness of their vocabulary.
- *Alternative treatment* Ask students to work in pairs and complete the phrases by looking at the definitions and from memory.
- 🎧 They then listen to check and complete their answers.

Answers
1 wild   2 captivity   3 occupation   4 logging
5 living   6 ideal   7 down   8 awareness
9 creatures

Extension idea Ask students to read the recording script on page 159 and underline or copy other useful words and phrases into their notebooks.

❹ *Alternative treatment* Ask students to select and use four or more phrases in their talks either from Exercise 3 or from the recording script on page 159.
- When students take turns to give their talks, the student who is listening can use the checklist on page 68 to give feedback to their partner at the end.

❺ Tell students that candidates who may achieve a high band score will be asked questions which ask them to speculate about the future, so at their level this is an essential ability.
- Point out that although some questions ask about the future explicitly, others do not. However, students can themselves volunteer ideas and opinions about the future when answering these questions as a way of giving a longer, more complete answer, and this will make a favourable impression on the examiner.

❻ 🎧

Answers
1 ahead; future   2 chance   3 likely   4 well
5 every   6 far   7 little   8 foreseeable

Extension idea Ask students to work in pairs and discuss what each phrase means, or when they would use it. (*Suggested answers:* **1** Looking into the future, I think the future for … will be good. **2** It's quite probable that … **3** It's very probable that … **4** It's quite probable that there will be … **5** It's possible that … **6** I think/believe …, but I may be wrong. **7** It's improbable that … **8** as far into the future as we can imagine or plan for.)
- Ask students to suggest other similar phrases. Write the most useful ones on the board for them to copy into their notebooks.

Note: now would be a good time to do the Key grammar on speculating and talking about the future.

❼ 🎧 Tell students they should first establish what each of the speakers' views are. Tell them to give reasons why they agree or disagree with each opinion expressed.

Note: now would be a good moment to do the Pronunciation section on word stress.

❽ *Alternative treatment* Ask students to work alone and choose one of the questions. Ask them to:
- look at the recording script on page 159 and write an answer which imitates the structure of one of the answers in the recording script
- include vocabulary and structures which they have studied in this section
- think about the pronunciation of the words they are going to use.
- When they are ready, ask them to work in small groups and read their answers to each other.
- When a student has read their answer, the other students should say:
  - which question was being answered
  - to what extent they agree or disagree with the answer.
- When they have finished, ask them to take turns to ask and answer the remaining questions.

Pronunciation Word stress

❶ *As a warmer* Write these phrases on the board: *an important point; the government was impotent in the situation; a large increase; numbers will increase.*
- Ask students where stress should be placed in the underlined words (im'portant, 'impotent, 'increase, in'crease). Point out how misplacing word stress can make one word sound like another.
- Go through the introduction to this section with students.
- Emphasise that the 'rules' they are going to study are indicators of where stress is likely to fall in a word, but that in the end, they have to learn the pronunciation of each word when they come across it, as they cannot be referring to rules when speaking.
- Tell students that a good learner's dictionary (such as the *Cambridge Advanced Learner's Dictionary* (*CALD*)) can be used as a reference for pronunciation: it gives a phonetic transcription, indicates which syllable(s) are stressed and, in the case of the *CALD*, provides a CD ROM with all words recorded with British and US pronunciation. These features are also available online at http://dictionary.cambridge.org.
- 🎧 When students do this exercise in the book, you may need to play the recording several times for students to check their answers.
- *Alternative treatment* Ask students to also check their answers to the first question by referring to a learner's dictionary.

> **Answers**
> 1 'certain 'species sur'vive pro'tect
>   'giant 'panda
> 2 1 first 2 second

Extension idea Discuss briefly with students how word stress differs from sentence stress. (*Answer:* Word stress refers to syllables which receive more or less stress in words of more than one syllable and are a fixed feature of each individual word; sentence stress is variable and depends on the particular emphasis the speaker chooses to place in the sentence. When a word is stressed in a sentence, the internal word stress remains the same.)

❷ 🎧

> **Answers**
> 1 Although the elephants were in cap'tivity, they used to be an im'portant part of the 'workforce in the forests – that was their 'primary occu'pation, but as a result of conser'vation programmes, there's less logging 'nowadays.
> 2 1 first 2 same 3 before 4 two

Extension idea Ask students to work in pairs and take turns to read the extract from Daeng's talk.

Key grammar
Speculating and talking about the future

❶ *As a warmer* Ask students in small groups to discuss: *What, for you, is more important: the past or the future? Why?*

> **Answers**
> 1 a 2 b 3 c

❷ When students have finished the exercise, go through the Language reference on page 118 with them.
- Ask them to record any useful phrases and collocations in their notebooks.
- Point out that using these phrases and collocations correctly and appropriately in both the Speaking and Writing papers is highly likely to increase their band score for those papers.

> **Answers**
> 1 b 2 c 3 c 4 a 5 b 6 c 7 a 8 b

❸ *Extension idea* Ask students to work alone and write three or four predictions of their own using the phrases in bold from Exercise 2.
- They then read their phrases aloud to their groups, who discuss to what extent they agree.

Writing Task 1

❶ *As a warmer* With books closed, tell students that this is the last point in the book with work on Writing Task 1. Ask them to work in small groups and think of good advice/exam techniques for answering this task.

- When they have finished, ask them to do the exercise in the book. Ask them if they thought of any other advice which is not included in this exercise.
- *Alternative treatment* While they are doing the exercise in the book, ask them to say why each of the points (1–10) is a good idea.

> **Answers**
> **2** diagram **3** task **4** key **5** paragraphs
> **6** figures **7** comparisons **8** overview
> **9** grammar and spelling **10** words

❷ Tell students that sometimes they will have to write a summary based on information from two or more sources. Tell them:

- there is always a relationship between the information in the different charts/diagrams
- there may be more to say about one chart/diagram than the other(s)
- data from both charts may need to be combined and/or compared in the answer in order to deal with the task successfully in the time available
- there is no right or wrong order in which to deal with the charts/diagrams, but students should decide on a **logical** order.
- Ask them to change partners and compare and discuss their plans.
- When they have finished, discuss and round up with the whole class, including discussing the relative merits of different plans.

> **Answers**
> **1** Both charts are about endangered plant species. The pie chart gives the proportions of plant species in danger, and the bar chart is about where they grow.
> **2** the size of the overall percentage of threatened plants; the proportion that are seriously in danger; the significant percentage of habitat loss in the tropics versus the very small percentage in the desert
> **3** Some of the levels of danger can be combined, and some of the areas can be combined under headings such as 'forest', 'grassland' and 'wetland'.
> **4** Suggested answer: four paragraphs
> 1) introduction; 2) pie chart; 3) bar chart;
> 4) overview
> **5** a reference to the size of habitat loss in the tropics and the fact that some plant species need immediate protection

❸ • Elicit why paragraphs and commas are important (*answer*: paragraphs help to clearly structure the piece, so the reader can follow the main points one by one; commas divide up sentences into groups of meaning where otherwise they might be confused). Point out that candidates cannot achieve a score above Band 7 for coherence and cohesion if they do not divide their Task 1 answer into paragraphs.

- *Alternative treatment* Before students insert the commas, ask them to read page 121 of the Language reference and use it to help them place the commas correctly.

> **Answers**
> The charts provide information on the proportion of plant species that are at risk, the levels of risk, and the different environments in which these plants grow. Although a lot of plants are safe, about a third of all plant species around the world are under some kind of threat. For just over 10 percent of these species, the threat is severe, with 3.92 percent of plants likely to become extinct and over 25 percent being vulnerable to extinction.
>
> When you look at plant habitats, the area with the greatest proportion of threatened species is tropical rainforest, where 63 percent of species are threatened. In contrast, desert areas have the lowest proportion of vulnerable plants at 0.5 percent. Forest grassland and wetland areas are also home to threatened species. However, the danger is on a much smaller scale than in the tropics, with figures ranging between 12 and one percent. To conclude, tropical areas of the world have more endangered plant species than others, and certain plants need immediate protection.

❹ **Answers**
1 with figures reaching
2 with costs going up
3 with teenage groups becoming
4 with numbers predicted to continue to fall
5 with the highest number being recorded
6 with 9.7 percent of land being over-used.

❺ *Alternative treatment* Ask students to briefly say what the function of each paragraph is. (*Suggested answers*: paragraph 1: what the charts show; paragraph 2: proportions of plants in danger; paragraph 3: areas where plants are in danger; paragraph 4: overview.)

6 *Alternative treatment* Ask students to think of synonyms for these words before looking back at the sample answer.

> **Answers**
> **1** at risk; under threat   **2** severe   **3** environments
> **4** home to   **5** on a much smaller scale

7 When they have finished discussing, ask students to compare their ideas with another pair of students.

> **Extension idea** Ask students in pairs to think of ways they can express the phrasing of the task using their own words. Remind students that it is important to use their own words as far as possible.

8 **Sample answer**
The data provide information about species extinctions in tropical forests and the reasons why plants become extinct.
Looking at the graph first, it can be seen that approximately 4,000 in every million species had become extinct by 2000. This figure is predicted to rise significantly until 2060, when it will hit a peak at 50,000 and then fall, though less steeply, to 28,000 per million in the year 2100.
The chart takes a close look at the impact of different types of activity on plant survival. Clearly, over three-quarters of extinctions are caused by human activity, and more than half of this is related in some way to farming. Other activities, such as logging (9.7 percent) and development (10.4 percent), also pose threats.
Natural events, on the other hand, have a much smaller effect on the lives of plants. Natural disasters, such as tropical storms, account for 7 percent of extinctions, while other natural influences cause a further 11.7 percent.
To sum up, extinctions in tropical regions will get much worse before they eventually fall. Meanwhile, human beings are likely to be responsible for the greater part of these.

Unit 7 photocopiable activity
Nature's future
Time: 50 minutes

Objectives

- To revise and practise grammatical structures for speculating and talking about the future
- To raise awareness of the importance of synonyms
- To recycle vocabulary related to the natural world
- To check students' awareness of word stress

Before class

Make one photocopy of the worksheet on page 100 for each pair of students. Cut it into two parts, so that half of the students have 'Student A' cards and the other half have 'Student B' cards.

1 *As a warmer* Write these three headings on the board: *certainty*; *probability*; *improbability*. Ask students to brainstorm phrases or grammatical forms which could be used to express each one. To help students get the idea, ask them which category would be best for this phrase: *It is highly likely that …* (probability).

> **Suggested answers**
> certainty: *There is no doubt that …*
> probability: *It is quite possible that …; There is a strong likelihood that …*
> improbability: *It is highly unlikely that …; There is little likelihood of …*

2 Divide the class into two groups, A and B. Give a 'Student A' card to all the students in Group A; all the students in Group B receive a 'Student B' card.

3 Focus students on the statements on their cards. Students work alone to complete their predictions for each statement in the table with *C* (certain), *P* (probable) or *I* (improbable). Encourage them to also add more predictions of their own in spaces 8–10.

4 Get students to compare their answers in pairs with a student from the same group. Ask them to talk for at least two minutes about each point using the language from the Warmer, giving their partner full explanations of the decisions they have made. Go round and monitor, paying particular attention to errors in word stress.

5 Once students have discussed their predictions, elicit reasons why it is important for IELTS candidates to know more than one way of expressing the same idea (*suggested answers*: a range of vocabulary to achieve a high band score; importance of paraphrasing questions in both Speaking and Writing tests; role of parallel expressions in Reading and Listening sections). Ask each pair to write down at least one synonym for each **bold** word or phrase on their card. Do not get feedback at this stage.

6 Now ask students to work in A/B pairs. First, they check the synonyms from step 5 by matching their **bold** words and phrases with the matching synonym on their partner's card. For example, the bold items in the first statements (*crack down on* and *take measures against*) are synonyms. The bold items in statements 2–7 match in a similar way.

7 Working in the same A/B pairs, students now take turns to give a three-minute report on their predictions from their previous discussion, and the reasons behind them, using appropriate language for speculating and talking about the future. Their partners can interrupt to ask for explanation or clarification of the points made.

8 When students have finished, conduct a feedback session with the whole class, during which you could ask students to share some of their predictions. You may also wish to give some feedback on the use of stress.

Extension idea Set this Writing task. Encourage students to use language from the previous activity.

> Write about the following topic.
>
> *Some people believe that the condition of the natural world will deteriorate steadily in future years due to pollution and other human factors. Others argue that current levels of conservation will be maintained and that natural habitats will be preserved.*
>
> *Discuss both views and give your opinion.*
>
> Give reasons for your answer and include any relevant examples from your own knowledge or experience.
>
> Write at least 250 words.

Unit 7 photocopiable activity
Nature's future

Student A: The future of living things

Write *C* (certain), *P* (probable) or *I* (improbable) next to each statement.

1	International authorities will manage to **crack down on** illegal practices such as smuggling animal skins.	
2	Humans will fail to **take into account** the need to protect wild animals, and as a result, animals will only survive on farms or in captivity.	
3	Despite changes in underwater temperatures, the oceans will remain a safe **habitat** for marine organisms.	
4	There will be a **critical** shortage of food in future, which will lead to international conflict.	
5	The number of plant and animal species which are currently **endangered** will decrease by the end of this century.	
6	Human life will be increasingly **under threat** due to the appearance of new, more dangerous viruses.	
7	Scientific discoveries will **improve understanding** of genetics, resulting in animals commonly being cloned for commercial purposes.	
8		
9		
10		

--------- ✂ --

Student B: The future of the wider environment

Write *C* (certain), *P* (probable) or *I* (improbable) next to each statement.

1	Governments will be forced to **take measures against** wasteful behaviour in the home, such as leaving lights on.	
2	Most countries will seriously **consider** the use of alternative sources of energy, such as wind or wave power.	
3	The countryside will increasingly be covered by urban development and will no longer be a protected **environment**.	
4	The number of **severe** accidents, such as oil spills or nuclear contamination, will decrease over the next century.	
5	Rivers and lakes will be less **vulnerable** to pollution because governments will agree new international laws to protect them.	
6	Communities in many areas will be **at risk** due to an increase in extreme weather events, such as storms and flooding.	
7	The international community will successfully **raise awareness** of the need to take action to protect the environment.	
8		
9		
10		

Word list

Unit 7

absorption *n* [U] (78) the process by which something is taken in and becomes part of something else

at risk *phrase* (82) being in a situation where something bad is likely to happen

blow *n* [C] (77) a shock or disappointment

bolster *v* [T] (78) to make something stronger by supporting it or encouraging it

check something out *vp* [T] (RS) to get more information about something by examining it or reading about it

cloning *n* [U] (81) the process of making an exact copy of a plant or animal by removing one of its cells

clue *n* [C] (77) a sign or piece of information that helps you to solve a problem or answer a question

culprit *n* [C] (78) something that is responsible for a bad situation

cultivate *v* [T] (78) to grow plants in large numbers

do/play your part *phrase* (78) to perform an important function

distinct *adj* (78) separate

diversity *n* [U] (78) when many different types of things or people exist

flora and fauna *phrase* (80) The flora and fauna of a place are its plants and animals.

forage *v* [I] (78) to move about searching for things you need, especially food

frighten someone off *vp* [T] (RS) to make a person or animal afraid so that they go away

fungal *adj* (78) caused by or relating to a fungus (= a type of organism which gets its food from decaying material or other living things)

go back to something *vp* [T] (77) to go back to a time in the past

greenhouse *n* [C] (77) a building made of glass for growing plants in

justification for something *np* [U] (80) a reason for something

longevity *n* [U] (78) living for a long time

menace *n* [C] (78) something that is likely to cause harm

microbes *plural n* (78) very small organisms, often bacteria that cause disease

monocrops *plural n* (78) single plants grown for food

numerous ways *phrase* (77) many different ways

on an international/global/national level *phrase* (78) If something is dealt with on an international/global/national, etc. level, it is dealt with by all the countries of the world or by a whole country.

parasite infestations *plural n* (78) when animals or plants that live on or in another type of animal cause problems by being somewhere in large numbers

pathogens *plural n* (78) small living things that can cause disease

read up on something *vp* [T] (RS) to read a lot about a subject in order to get information

setback *n* [C] (77) a problem that makes something happen later or more slowly than it should

stunning *adj* (76) very beautiful

tease something apart *vp* [T] (78) to separate different things

tempt *v* [T] (RS) to make you want to do or have something

thrive *v* [I] (78) to grow very well, or to become very healthy or successful

toxic *adj* (78) poisonous

under threat *phrase* (82) If something is under threat, it is in danger.

vicinity *singular n* (78) the area near a place

viral *adj* (78) caused by or relating to a virus (= infectious organism)

Vocabulary extension

Unit 7

abundant *adj* existing in large quantities

animal and plant life *phrase* living things, both animals and plants

biodiversity *n* [U] the number and types of plant and animal species that exist in a particular environmental area, or in the world generally

biological clock *n* [C] the body's natural habit of sleeping, eating, growing, etc. at particular times

capture an image *vp* [T] to record someone or something on camera

close-up *n* [C] a photograph of someone or something that is taken by standing very close to them

conservation issues *plural n* problems relating to the protection of nature, especially from the damaging effects of human activity

ecosystem *n* [C] all the living things in an area and the way they affect each other and the environment

emit *v* [T] to send out gas, heat, light, etc. into the air

enforce a law *vp* [T] to make people obey laws

the Forestry Commission *n* singular the government department in the UK which is responsible for protecting and increasing Britain's forests and other areas of land with trees

fundamental differences *plural n* very basic, important differences

in captivity *np* If an animal is in captivity, it is kept somewhere and not allowed to leave.

intensive agriculture *np* [U] a way of farming which produces the largest quantity of crops and meat for the smallest area of land and requires large quantities of water, pesticides (= chemicals for killing insects) and fertilisers (= substances for making plants grow)

invertebrate *n* [C] an animal with no spine (= bones in the back), for example an insect

life cycle *np* [C] the changes that happen during the different stages of an animal's or a plant's life

livestock *n* [U] animals that are kept on a farm

nature versus nurture *phrase* the relative importance of the characteristics that a person was born with ('nature') and the characteristics that a person develops as a result of their experiences in life ('nurture')

nutrient *n* [C] formal any substance that an animal needs to eat and a plant needs from the soil in order to live and grow

pest *n* [C] an animal that causes damage to plants, food, etc.

pose a threat *vp* [T] to be likely to cause harm to something or someone

resistant *adj* not harmed or affected by something

sector *n* [C] one of the parts that a chart is divided into

soil fertility *n* [U] the ability of the soil to produce a lot of healthy plants

susceptible to something *adj* easily harmed by something

sustainable farming *np* [U] farming that uses methods that do not damage the environment

swarm *n* [C] a large group of creatures, usually insects, moving together

vertebrate *n* [C] an animal with a spine (= bones in the back), for example a mammal or a bird

virtually extinct *phrase* If a type of animal or plant is virtually extinct, very few of them now exist on Earth.

vulnerable to something *adj* easily harmed by something

 Complete IELTS Bands 6.5–7.5 by Guy Brook-Hart and Vanessa Jakeman with David Jay © Cambridge University Press 2013

Unit 8　Across the universe

Unit objectives

- **Reading Section 3:** skimming; dealing with references; time management in the test; Yes / No / Not Given; multiple choice; summary completion
- **Vocabulary:** verbs and dependent prepositions
- **Listening Section 4:** note completion
- **Speaking Parts 2 and 3:** round-up of exam technique; expressions about the past; contrasting past and present; speculating about the future,
- **Pronunciation:** rhythm and chunking
- **Writing Task 2:** analysing the question; brainstorming; dealing with two questions; writing a conclusion
- **Key grammar:** emphasising

Starting off

As a warmer With books closed and students in groups, tell them: *This unit is about space and the universe. If you were going to choose five photos to illustrate an exhibition called 'Our place in space', what types of image would you choose?*

- **Alternative treatment** If you did *As a warmer*, with books open ask students whether the photos they thought of were similar to or different from the photos in the book.

Suggested answers
1 1 China's first manned space docking mission, including the first Chinese female astronaut (June 2012)
  2 when humans first stepped on the Moon
  3 the use of robots to explore Mars
  4 The International Space Station: the first international collaboration in space (first component was launched in 1998)
  5 the use of the Hubble Space Telescope to explore the universe
  6 Yuri Gagarin, the first man in space (1961)
2 1 showed China's commitment to the exploration of space / marked a significant point in Chinese history
  2 established possibility of research on the Moon / other Moon landings
  3 looks for signs of life on Mars / information that might help scientists understand Earth better
  4 enabled countries to pool resources / provides a centre for research

  5 can see further than any Earth-based telescope / orbits the Earth / makes discoveries, such as age of universe, how galaxies form, etc.
  6 confirmed that humans could travel safely into space / began the exploration of space / led to further space missions and the Moon landing

Extension idea Ask students in small groups: *Do you think there are any negative aspects to space exploration? What are they?*

Reading　Section 3

❶ *As a warmer* With books closed, tell students that they are going to do Reading Section 3. Elicit from or tell them that:
  – this is usually the hardest section of the Reading paper
  – it has 14, not 13 questions
  – it should take 20 minutes to do.
- Ask students how they can allow sufficient time for Reading Section 3. (*Answer:* By managing their time carefully on the previous two sections.)
- Tell them that unless they give Section 3 sufficient time, they will severely limit their chances of achieving a high band score.
- Elicit also that they should:
  – glance at the tasks before they start reading
  – check the title and any subheading
  – skim the passage quickly in about two minutes.

Suggested answer
It unites humans in a common goal. It means that more money is available and the best resources/ equipment, etc. can be used. It avoids duplication of effort and unnecessary competition.

Extension idea Ask:
 – *What role do you think a charity might have in space?*
 – *Do you think people will one day live on other planets?*
 – *Do you think their nationality will be important if and when they do this?*

❷ Tell students that just looking at the types of question may affect how they skim the passage. For example, if they see there is a summary completion, they can look at the summary title and, when they skim the passage, notice where the subject of the title is dealt with in the passage. However, they should not read the questions in detail at this stage.

❸ *Alternative treatment* This passage does not have a subheading. When students have finished skimming the passage, ask them to work in pairs and suggest a subheading. (*Suggested answer:* A charity brings Earth exploration and space exploration together.)

❹ When students have finished discussing the questions, summarise with the whole class. The following points should emerge:
– The answers for questions in each task type will come in the same order in the passage as the questions. However, when students start a new task, for example the multiple-choice Questions 6–9, they may have to scan again from the beginning of the passage to find the answers.
– **Yes / No / Not Given** questions contain key words which will be the same or similar to words in the passage. Students should identify these words when they read each question and scan to find where they are dealt with in the passage, then read carefully from there.
– Yes / No / Not Given questions usually deal with the views or claims of the writer, whereas True / False / Not Given questions tend to deal with information or facts.
– For the answer 'No', the passage will contradict the question; for the answer 'Not Given', there will be nothing in the passage about exactly what the statement says.
– For **multiple-choice** questions, students should read the question (or stem), then scan the passage to find where it is dealt with. They read that part of the passage carefully to understand the answer, then read options A–D and decide which one matches what they have understood from the passage.
– Students should quickly underline the words which give them the answers: this will confirm that there is evidence in the passage which supports their choices.
• There are 14 questions, and candidates have 18 minutes to answer them (having spent two minutes skimming the passage), so they should spend just over one minute on each question: tell students not to get bogged down on a question, but to keep up the pace to ensure they have time to answer everything. For Questions 1–9, they should probably spend 11–12 minutes.

• If you have agreed a time limit for Questions 1–9 (say 11 or 12 minutes), time the class and be strict about the timing.
• *Alternative treatment* When students have finished, they can work in pairs and compare their answers.

Answers
1 YES (... *despite the fact that both fields of interest involve what might be referred to as 'scientific exploration'.*)
2 NO (*The reason for this dichotomous existence is chiefly historical. The exploration of the Earth has been occurring over many centuries, and the institutions created to do it are often very different from those founded in the second part of the 20th century to explore space. This separation is also caused by the fact that space exploration has attracted experts from mainly non-biological disciplines – primarily engineers and physicists – but the study of Earth and its environment is a domain heavily populated by biologists.*)
3 NOT GIVEN (The text mentions governments and money, but nothing is said about how much they allocate to each type of research.)
4 NO (... *those involved in space exploration can provide the satellites to monitor the Earth's fragile environments, and environmentalists can provide information on the survival of life in extreme environments.*)
5 NOT GIVEN (The Foundation is mentioned, but there is nothing about the timing of its establishment.)
6 C (... *another approach is to enhance the value of the forests ... This novel approach is now making the protection of the forests a sensible economic decision.*)
7 A (... *to locate mounds, or 'tels', containing artefacts and remnants of early civilisations. These collections are being used to build a better picture of the nature of the civilisations that gave birth to astronomy.*)
8 D (... *they provide longevity for the objectives of the Foundation.*)
9 B (The writer's tone is explanatory; there are no requests for support, nothing has changed about the Foundation's work, and there is no reference to any criticisms of the Foundation's work.)

Extension ideas
1 Ask students how it felt to do the tasks alone (assuming they did this) and with a strict time limit.
• Elicit what they should do about questions that they struggle with (perhaps put a cross by them and return to them at the end if they have time, but not go over their time limit per question of just over a minute).

- Remind students that when they have finished, they should have answered every question, even if this has involved some guessing.

2 Ask students what key words they underlined in Questions 1–5 and if these helped them scan for the answers in the passages. (*Suggested underlining:*
   1 environmental protection / space exploration
   2 space exploration / environmental studies
   3 Governments / money **4** environmental and space exploration communities / resources
   5 Earth and Space Foundation / set up)

❺ Before students actually tackle the questions, round up their pre-task discussion. These points should emerge:

- They should use the summary title to find the part of the passage which contains the information.
- They should read before and after the gaps in the summary to ascertain what information they need.
- The order of the questions may be different from the order in which the answers will be found in the passage.
- Students should quickly read through the completed summary when they have finished to make sure it makes sense and reflects the information in the passage.
- This task of five questions should take them six to seven minutes, depending on how long they spent on Questions 1–9.
- Again, once a time limit has been agreed, be strict about keeping to it.

> **Answers**
> **10** B (*This may include the use of remote environments on Earth, as well as physiological and psychological studies in harsh environments.*)
> **11** H (*... to study the psychology of explorers subjected to long-term isolation in caves in Mexico.*)
> **12** A (*Space-like environments on Earth help us understand how to operate in the space environment or help us characterise extraterrestrial environments for future scientific research.*)
> **13** D (*The crater, which sits in high Arctic permafrost, provides an excellent replica of the physical processes occurring on Mars ...*)
> **14** G (*... and possibly biological potential of Mars.*)

❻ Remind students that they will need to find answers to questions across sentences, and that the ability to make connections, sometimes using references within the text, is an essential skill.

- *Alternative treatment* To hone students' scanning skills, give them two minutes to underline the phrases (1–6) in the passage. Tell them this is exactly the skill they need for finding the parts

of the passage to answer True / False / Not Given and Yes / No / Not Given tasks.

> **Answers**
> **1** the exploration of space and the study and/or protection of the Earth's environment; Q1
> **2** the divided nature of the two fields; Q2
> **3** the space exploration community and environmentalists; Q4
> **4** the artefacts and remnants of early civilisations; Q7
> **5** awards for expeditions on Mars and to other parts of the solar system; Q8

❼ *Extension idea* For some 'fun' questions, follow up with:
- *Would you like to visit another planet? Why? / Why not?*
- *What experiences would you hope for if you travelled in space?*
- *If you were to meet intelligent beings from another planet, what would you ask them?*

Vocabulary Verbs and dependent prepositions

❶ *As a warmer* Ask students: *How do you learn dependent prepositions? What techniques do you have for learning them?*
- From the ensuing discussion, it should emerge that students should:
  - learn them when they learn the verb itself
  - use dictionaries for reference when they are not sure which preposition to use
  - copy words and dependent prepositions into their notebooks, perhaps keeping a special section for them
  - try to use them when speaking and writing, as using them correctly will fix them in the memory.
- Tell students that correct use of dependent prepositions in their speaking and writing will help to raise their band scores.
- Ask them to answer the questions without looking at the passage. They can then check their answers by scanning the passage.
- Remind students that:
  - verbs may also be followed by infinitives or verb + –*ing*
  - verbs following prepositions will always use the –*ing* form
  - *to* may be part of the infinitive, or, as in the examples in this exercise, a preposition. If it is a preposition, any verb following it will use –*ing*.

- *Alternative treatment* Instead of checking their answers by scanning the passage again, ask students to check their answers by looking at the lists in the Language reference on page 123.

Answers
1 on   2 as   3 in   4 as; from   5 from   6 from

Extension idea Tell, or remind students that verbs with similar meanings are often (but not always) followed by the same preposition.

- Write these verbs on the board:
  arise, concentrate, divert, expose, originate, submit, think of
- Ask students to look for verbs in the exercise which have similar meanings to the verbs on the board (*answers:* result–arise; focus–concentrate; divert–distract; subject–expose; originate–stem; submit–subject; think–regard) and to say what dependent preposition each will have (*answers:* arise from; concentrate on; divert from; expose to; originate from; submit to; think of as).

❷ Ask students to answer these questions and then check their answers in the Language reference section on page 112.
- *Alternative treatment* Ask students to check their answers by using a dictionary, and in this way highlight the usefulness of dictionaries.

Answers
1 in; on   2 to   3 with   4 from   5 in   6 to   7 as

❸ *Alternative treatment* Ask students to work alone and write their answers. They can then compare their ideas with a partner or in small groups.

Suggested answers
Correct prepositions in bold
1 ... **to** people who are fascinated by the night sky.
2 ... **from** childhood experiences
3 ... **to** the landing of the robot on Mars.
4 ... **in** their views about the value of space exploration.
5 ... **with** the skills I need to set up my own business.
6 ... **as** the 'red planet'.
7 ... **on** the impact of their articles on the general public.

Listening   Section 4

❶ *As a warmer* With books closed, ask students:
- *How many sections does the Listening paper have?* (*answer:* four)
- *How many times do you hear each section?* (*answer:* once only)
- *Do you listen to each section without pauses?* (*Answer:* There are pauses between sections and pauses in the middle of Sections 1–3, but not in Section 4.)
- *What happens when the recording has stopped, but before the Listening paper finishes?* (*Answer:* You have some time to transfer your answers to the answer sheet.)

Answers
1 *decide what you need to listen for* (It is very important to make full use of all the preparation time. Use this time to underline key ideas.)
2 *listen for key ideas in the questions* (Use your underlining to help you find your place again.)
3 *matters* (When you transfer your answers onto an answer sheet, completion tasks must be grammatical and spelled correctly.)
4 *count*
5 *make a guess* (Even if you're not sure of an answer, guess and write something.)
6 *will* (Never go over the word limit. If you do, the answer will be marked wrong.)

❷ **Suggested answer**
Briefly, before Galileo, the Earth was considered by many to be the centre of the universe. After Galileo, the Sun was considered the centre. More recent observations have revealed the immense size of the universe and the billions of galaxies, each containing billions of stars.

Extension idea As a follow-up question, you can ask: *How has our developing understanding of space changed the way we see ourselves in the universe?*

❸ When students have finished discussing, ask them to look at the Exam advice boxes on pages 44 and 67. If necessary, elicit the steps outlined in the answers below.

Suggested answers
- Look at the title of the lecture or talk and how it is structured. There are three sections: the first is about space observation in the past, the second is about space observation today and the third is about amateur astronomers. The third part also has sub-sections on the knowledge of amateur observers, the types of observation they do, and the advantages of using them.
- Look at the gaps and decide what type of word and what information is missing. All the gaps, apart from 10 (which is an adjective or adjective phrase), are either nouns or noun phrases.
  1 describes an activity that was started by the first telescopes
  2 something that contrasts with *sky*
  3 a 'first' in space or in relation to space observation
  4 something astronomers want to find or look for
  5 the name of a beautiful image linked with Greece
  6 something about a space object that changes
  7 something that amateur astronomers can produce
  8 a type of discovery / something that can be discovered (beginning with a vowel)
  9 something to do with objects in space
  10 describes a type of observation

❹ 🎧 Play the recording once only.
- *Alternative treatment* To give students a feel for exam conditions, give them a few minutes to transfer their answers to their notebooks. While they do this, tell them to check that they have spelled their answers correctly. Ensure that they have answered every question.
- When they have finished, ask them to compare their answers with a partner.
- If you wish, play the recording again for them to check.

Answers
1 scientific revolution 2 (the) Earth / (the) earth
3 moon/Moon photo(graph)
4 research data 5 solar eclipse 6 brightness
7 accurate measurement(s) 8 exploding star
9 evolution 10 long(-)term

Extension idea Write these answers on the board and ask students to say which are correct and which are wrong. Where they are wrong, ask students to correct them:
1 sceintific revolution 2 on the Earth 3 moon photograph 4 researchs data 5 solar eclipse 6 brightness 7 measurements 8 an exploding star 9 evolution 10 long
- This activity should highlight the need for correct spelling, writing the most complete answer where possible, not exceeding the word limit, and writing grammatically correct answers.

❺ *Alternative treatment* Ask: *Do you think we will ever understand the origins of the universe? Why? / Why not?*

Speaking Parts 2 and 3

❶ *As a warmer* Ask students to work in small groups and discuss how they can prepare for the Speaking test beforehand and on the day.
- When you round up, if these ideas do not arise, elicit them:
  - Students should be able to speak confidently about themselves – they should know how to describe their jobs/studies, their home life and interests, their ambitions for the future.
  - They should practise speaking on subjects for two minutes in English and go into the Speaking test with that intention.
  - They should be ready to offer opinions and ideas on the more abstract topics raised in Part 3 and extend their answers.
  - On the day itself, they should arrive for the test in plenty of time. If possible, speak to another candidate in English before going to the Speaking test so that it is not the first time they have spoken English that day. They should look at the examiner and smile when introduced.
- When students answer the questions, remind them in relation to the fifth question, that they will be rated for the relevance of their answers, not their opinions, though obviously it is desirable in an exam with an examiner you do not know to avoid expressing extreme or silly opinions.

Answers
1 *about two or three sentences long* (Although Part 1 answers tend to be shorter than Part 3 answers, you still need to give some reasons and examples.)
2 *not have* (Tasks are designed to be straightforward and easy to talk about.)
3 *the full two minutes* (At this level, examiners will expect you to be able to speak for two minutes.)
4 *the same marks as* (See the Speaking reference (page 100) for more information on marking.)
5 *general and abstract*
6 *just as* (The four marking criteria are equally important.)
7 *will* (If your answer is irrelevant, you will get no credit for it.)

2 Remind students particularly to note down advanced vocabulary they can use when giving their talk.

3 When students have finished, ask them to compare their ideas for the checklist with the rest of the class. Then refer them to previous checklists on pages 36 and 68.

Suggested answers
address all the bullet points; refer to your notes and/or the task; use techniques to paraphrase and/or avoid hesitation; use relevant and appropriate vocabulary; use some advanced vocabulary; use a range of linkers/discourse markers to structure your talk and join ideas; use accurate grammar; round off your talk

Extension idea After giving each other feedback, ask students to change partners and give their talks again, putting into practice the feedback they received.
- If you feel they are becoming tired of the topic, ask them to prepare and give similar talks where the topic is: *Describe a journey that you have read about or seen in a film or on TV.*

4 Tell students that in the exam itself, they should expect to answer at least three questions, because examiners will ask a number of follow-up questions, depending on what and how much the candidate says.

Answers
1 c (possibly a or b)   2 c   3 a and c   4 b and c

Extension idea Ask students to work in pairs and brainstorm phrases they have studied in this course for each point a–c.
- When they have finished, they should check by looking at pages 58 (reasons and examples) and 81 (speculation).

5 🎧
Answers
1 a and c   2 c   3 a, b and c   4 b and c

6 **Answers**
a It goes right back to; it's like the time when; Over the centuries; we know a great deal more; we still know relatively little; Back in the 1960s; we've reached the point now where
b it's unlikely that; there's little point in; governments may well continue
c reasons: because; since; At a time when examples: It goes right back to; it's like the time when; so there are … there are … and then there are …

Extension idea Ask students to copy useful words and phrases into their notebooks.
- Then ask them to look at the questions from Exercise 4 on page 90 and approximately reconstruct Pauline's answers to the questions using some of the phrases and her ideas.

Note: this would be a good time to do the Pronunciation work on rhythm and chunking.

7 ***Alternative treatment*** Ask students to work in pairs. One student should close their book. The other student should take the part of the examiner, but ask the questions in a random order.
- He/She can use the checklist to give feedback where necessary.
- When they have finished, students should change roles and ask and answer the questions again.

8 Ask students to change partners for this final exercise.
- ***Alternative treatment*** Ask students to look at the fixed phrases they worked on in the Pronunciation section (assuming they have done it by now).
- Ask them to incorporate some of the phrases into their answers as they answer the questions.

Pronunciation Rhythm and chunking

1 🎧 ***Alternative treatment*** With books closed, ask students to listen and say which words/syllables are stressed. They should then repeat the phrases.

2 **Answers**
1 I've <u>no</u> <u>i</u>dea
2 <u>What</u>'s the <u>point</u>?
3 make <u>both</u> ends <u>meet</u>
4 It's <u>like</u> the <u>time</u> when …
5 on the <u>other</u> <u>hand</u>
6 <u>o</u>ver the <u>years</u>

Extension idea Ask students to write two or three sentences using some of these phrases. They then read the sentences aloud, keeping the rhythm in the set phrases.

❸ Answers
1 <u>Well</u>, it's <u>hard</u> to <u>say</u>. I think that, **over the decades**, people have **lost interest**.
2 You <u>know</u>, if you **go** <u>back</u> to the <u>time</u> of Galileo, no one even <u>thought</u> about travelling into space then.
3 **As far as** <u>space</u> is <u>concerned</u>, I don't think we have <u>any</u> <u>idea</u> what's out there.
4 A <u>lot</u> of people say '<u>What's</u> the <u>point</u> in space exploration?', but **as** <u>far</u> as <u>I</u> can see, that's a <u>bit</u> **short**-<u>sighted</u>.
5 Actually, <u>I</u> <u>can't</u> <u>wait</u> to <u>see</u> what the Mars robot **comes** <u>up</u> with. I think **the** <u>whole space</u> thing is just <u>out</u> of this <u>world</u>!

❹ Extension idea If they didn't do the Alternative treatment in Speaking Exercise 8, ask students to write an answer to a question from Speaking Exercise 4 using some of the fixed phrases from Pronunciation Exercise 3.
• They then practise reading their answers aloud.
• Finally, they work in pairs and without reading, they take turns to say their sentences.

Writing Task 2

❶ *As a warmer* With books closed, ask students to work in small groups and discuss what advice they would give for achieving a high band score in Writing Task 2; for example, analyse the question/task carefully.
• Round up with the whole class. Then ask them to open their books and complete the exercise.
• Ask students if there is any advice here they didn't think of.

Answers
2 questions   3 plan; main ideas   4 sentences
5 vocabulary   6 view   7 grammar and spelling

Extension idea Ask students to give reasons for each piece of advice, for example: *Leave 40 minutes to complete the task because you will need it to deal with the task adequately and write 250 words. Also, it carries twice the number of marks of Task 1, which should take 20 minutes.*

❷ When they have finished discussing, round up with the whole class.
• Point out that:
  – a common pitfall is to concentrate on one of the questions and not deal with or give enough weight to the other. Students should deal with each part of the task fully; failure to do so may

result in a good candidate only scoring a Band 5 for task response
  – where the task says *include any relevant examples from your own knowledge or experience*, here they will probably not have personal experience and it is not necessary to include this in their answer, so they should include examples from their knowledge where possible.
• *Alternative treatment* Ask students to underline the key ideas in the task as they read it.

Answers
1 There are two questions: the first requires a view on the statement with reasons and examples; the second requires some predictions about the impact.

Extension idea Ask students to write a plan for this task.

❸ Remind students that it is very clear to examiners when essays have not been planned: they are liable to be disorganised, lack coherence and therefore lose marks, so it is essential that students spend a few minutes planning before they start writing.

Suggested answer
Paragraph 1: my view – it's very true / people have desire / need the means
Paragraph 2: first question – people have some means now / some people have been / more will follow / natural tendency to want to do this
Paragraph 3: businesses developing further / example, Richard Branson
Paragraph 4: second question – business and exploration are separate / will not influence each other
Paragraph 5: counter-argument – could raise money / channel this back into space exploration

Extension ideas
1 Ask students: *To what extent do you agree with the writer's views?*
2 Ask students:
  – *What is missing from this essay?* (answer: a concluding paragraph)
  – *What would you expect to see in the concluding paragraph?*
• Ask students to work alone and write their own concluding paragraph for this essay.
• If you do this extension idea, it may be a good idea to do Exercise 5 before you do Exercise 4.

❹ Remind students that they will gain extra marks by linking their ideas clearly and writing a coherent, well-organised essay.

> **Answers**
> 1 at the start of the fourth paragraph; by asking an indirect question (*How that will change space exploration is an interesting question.*)
> 2 by using referencing (*that means* (paragraph 2); *that* (paragraph 4)); by comparing (*In the same way* (paragraph 3)); by introducing a counter-argument (*Having said that* (paragraph 5))

Extension ideas

1 Ask students in pairs to reread the essay, underlining all the referencing devices and to say what each refers to, e.g. 'them' in Paragraph 1 refers to wealthy people, etc.

2 • Write these words/phrases on the board: *to a certain extent; in fact; so; essentially; in turn.*
   • Ask students: *What is the function of each of these words/phrases in the essay?* (*Answers:* **to a certain** extent – to say this situation already exists in part, but not completely; **in fact** – to emphasise the point made in the previous sentence by adding an extra detail; **so** – to introduce a conclusion being drawn from the previous point; **essentially** – to emphasise that by their nature they are not the same; **in turn** – to say that this will lead to a further consequence.)
   • Tell students to copy the words/phrases into their notebooks and point out that using phrases like these in the exam will give the examiner a positive impression.
   • Ask students to write their own sentences using these words/phrases. When they have finished, ask some students to read their sentences to the whole class and comment on how well they have been used.

❺ **Answers**
2 1 b   2 c   3 a

Extension idea If you did Extension idea 2 from Exercise 3, ask students to exchange the concluding paragraphs they wrote with another partner. Ask them to write or give a 'teacher's comment' about their partner's conclusion; they can take ideas from the teacher's comments in this exercise.

❻ **Answers**
1 the means (to)   2 a natural tendency (to)
3 push the boundaries   4 setting their sights (on something)   5 only a matter of time (before)
6 as time goes by   7 a regular occurrence
8 (only) time will tell   9 seeking
10 contributing to

❼ **Answers**
1 only a matter of time   2 push the boundaries
3 natural tendency/tendencies
4 set his sights on   5 the means

Note: now would be a good time to do the Key grammar on emphasising.

❽ Tell students that before they do the Writing task, they should look back through the unit (and their notebooks) and assemble vocabulary and phrases which they would find useful for writing this essay.
• Tell them they can take time to do this, but that they should only spend 40 minutes writing the plan, writing the essay and checking it afterwards.

> **Sample answer**
> It is only in the last century that humans have explored space and, to begin with, nations established their space programmes independently. However, this situation has changed over time, and I believe the spirit of co-operation which is now more common is likely to continue into the future, although some competition will remain.
> One reason why nations worked alone on their space technology was that governments were not used to international collaboration and did not have the relationships that they do today. In particular, Russia and North America regarded space exploration as a race that they had to win, rather than an opportunity to work together.
> Another reason is that nations, like individuals, are naturally competitive, and space exploration offers an opportunity for countries to take pride in their successes and achievements. Thus Russia was able to celebrate Yuri Gagarin's memorable flight into space in 1961, while the US enjoyed the thrilling sight of Neil Armstrong walking on the Moon in 1969.
> Since that time, the space race has slowed down, and there has been more emphasis on research, with robots and shuttles doing the work of manned spacecraft. These days, fewer astronauts have to risk their lives, and there is less need for one nation to try to get ahead of another. Instead, there is collaboration, including the development of the International Space Station, one of the greatest space projects in history.
> Having said that, the universe is vast and much remains to be explored. We have yet to land an astronaut on Mars, for example, and new planets are being discovered all the time. While there are still 'firsts' to be won, it is probable that some national programmes will remain, such as the Chinese space project in my country, which aims to explore Mars over the next few years.

Thus the picture in the future looks mixed. I believe that nations will work together in many areas, but I also feel that a natural rivalry between countries will continue.

Key grammar Emphasising

❶ *As a warmer* Tell students that they are going to work on using emphatic devices. Ask them, in pairs, to look back at the sample answer in Exercise 3 and highlight any emphatic devices they can find.
- They should then look at the exercise in the book and compare the sentences (1–3) with their answers.

> **Answers**
> 1 is   2 that   3 where

Extension idea To highlight the concept of emphasis, ask students to rewrite the three sentences in an unemphatic way and to compare the effect. (*Suggested answers:* **1** These people just need the means to achieve their aims. **2** This desire to push boundaries has motivated every explorer in the past. / Every explorer in the past has been motivated by this desire to push boundaries. **3** In the same way, business people in the travel industry are setting their sights on space.)

❷ When students have finished doing this exercise, go through the Language reference on page 112 with them.

> **Answers**
> 1 *all* – that this is the only thing needed
> 2 *desire* – this particular one   3 *space* – the place

❸ Tell students that there may be more than one possible answer to some of these questions.

> **Answers**
> 1 It was Yuri Gagarin who was the first man in space, not Neil Armstrong.
> 2 What the ISS shows is how successfully nations can co-operate. / What shows how successfully nations can co-operate is the ISS.
> 3 Mars is considered (by some people) to be the most interesting planet.
> 4 It is the sense of weightlessness that I would find rather unnerving.
> 5 Clearly this picture is the best (one) / is better than any of the others we will get/take.
> 6 What he does is (to) spend long hours in his observatory. / What long hours he spends in his observatory!
> 7 It's only millionaires who can afford to travel into space. / It's millionaires who are the only people who can afford to travel into space.

❹ Ask students to compare their answers to these questions in small groups and to read out answers which they think are particularly good or interesting to the whole class.

> **Suggested answers**
> 1 It wasn't me who broke the equipment, it was my sister.
> 2 He's a great violinist. What he does is to practise for six hours every day.
> 3 What you need to do is to break some of the habits that you've established over a lifetime.
> 4 What it taught me is that patience is the best way to deal with tired children.
> 5 The Moon is generally believed to have an influence on our moods.

Vocabulary and grammar review
Unit 7

> **Answers**
> 1 cloud, ant(s), green, prey, sky, tree(s), cat, sun, bull, rainbow(s)

B	J	C	L	O	U	D	E	R
T	U	A	N	T	S	U	A	S
R	S	L	I	S	L	I	O	U
E	C	R	L	D	N	O	F	N
E	A	A	L	B	L	T	H	E
S	T	K	O	G	R	E	E	N
I	N	W	G	O	P	R	E	Y
F	S	C	R	S	K	Y	E	A

> 2 **2** bull; b   **3** sky; e   **4** cloud; f   **5** trees; a
> **6** rainbows; d
> 3 *Suggested answers*
> **1** The government has given the green light to the local council to build a new hospital.
> **2** If you work hard and pass all your exams, the sky is the limit.
> **3** There were so many pages to/in the report that we couldn't see the wood for the trees.
> 4 **2** probably   **3** could   **4** likely   **5** are
> **6** will be   **7** chance
> 5 Ants, which form natural groups called ant colonies, have much to teach us about group behaviour. As individuals, ants are not the most intelligent of creatures. However, when they get into groups, they are seen to behave in very intelligent ways.

If you look at how ants gather food, for example, you can quickly see how the group mentality works. Rather than all rushing out at once, a few foragers do the first trip. Having found food, they return to the nest and send a signal to other ants to go out. Ants don't sit and decide how many foragers they need first, which means that they can quickly adapt if a predator is around.

Ultimately, no one ant realises what it is doing on its own, but each ant's actions are connected to those of other ants. Could such a lack of central control work in business? Definitely, says one expert!

Unit 8

Answers

1 2 with   3 to   4 from   5 of
   6 on   7 with   8 from   9 as

2 2 temperature   3 opportunities   4 countries
   5 exercise   6 nowadays   7 competition
   8 dropped   9 happened   10 different

3 2 Essentially   3 time will tell   4 push the
   boundaries   5 speed up   6 in the long run

4 1 What people want are solutions to the problems
      on Earth.
   2 Astronomy is the scientific study of the universe,
      not astrology. / Astronomy, not astrology, is the
      scientific study of the universe.
   3 It is only in the last hundred years that humans
      have ventured into space.
   4 Regardless of the risk, space travel
      fascinates me.
   5 All we / that was needed to enhance our
      knowledge of the universe was a greater level of
      international co-operation.
   6 What we did was to stay up all night observing
      the stars.

Unit 8 photocopiable activity
Extraterrestrial ethics   Time: 60 minutes

Objectives

- To practise the use of grammatical structures for emphasising
- To revise verbs and dependent prepositions
- To raise awareness of rhythm and chunking
- To practise spoken fluency in a presentation format

Before class

Make one photocopy of the worksheet on page 114 for each student.

1 *As a warmer* Ask students whether they think life exists on other planets. If so, what form would it take?

2 Give each student a copy of the worksheet. Students work in pairs or groups of three to do Exercise 1. Check answers with the class.

Answers

1 on   2 on   3 in   4 with   5 as   6 in   7 from
8 to

3 Move on to Exercise 2 on the worksheet. Be ready to help if needed. If students have difficulty completing the task, you may wish to revise the structures for emphasising in Unit 8 of the Student's Book.

Suggested answers

1   It is our long-term goal that we have to focus on.
2   What we need to reflect on is the possible outcome of our actions.
3   All we have to believe in is the power of communication.
4   A hostile reaction is what we may have to cope with.
5   Safety is what we regard as the most important factor.
6   What we do not want to be involved in is any aggressive activity.
7   It is greed that could distract us from our true objectives.
8   What they will never agree to is permanent colonisation.

4 Ask students to look at the picture and read the scenario on the worksheet. Each pair or group must prepare a five-minute presentation covering all of the discussion points on the worksheet. It is up to each group to decide who will address each point, as long as every group member has an equal chance to speak at length. The group which gives the most convincing presentation will be allowed to lead the Zeta 4 project.

5 Remind students to use the emphatic language from Exercise 2 to help them strengthen their arguments. Give the groups as much time as they need to prepare their presentation, helping if needed.

6 During the presentations, monitor for errors in the use of emphatic language and dependent prepositions. You may also wish to check the students' control of rhythm and chunking.

7 Once all the groups have presented, conduct a class vote to see who will lead the project. Encourage students to vote honestly based on the arguments they have heard, rather than just for their own group.

8 After the voting, conduct a feedback session, based on any errors you noticed in Step 6. Write these on the board for students to discuss and correct in pairs. It is also a good idea to praise some examples of effective language use, to keep the feedback balanced.

Extraterrestrial ethics

❶ Complete the sentences below with the correct preposition from the box.

| as from in in on on to with |

1 We have to focus .... **our long-term goal.**
2 We need to reflect .... **the possible outcome of our actions.**
3 We have to believe .... **the power of communication.**
4 We may have to cope .... **a hostile reaction.**
5 We regard safety .... **the most important factor.**
6 We do not want to be involved .... **any aggressive activity.**
7 Greed could distract us .... **our true objectives.**
8 They will never agree .... **permanent colonisation.**

❷ Rewrite the sentences in Exercise 1 so that the ideas in bold are emphasised.

1 It is …
2 What we …
3 All we have …
4 A hostile reaction is …
5 Safety is …
6 What we …
7 It is …
8 What they …

The year is 2250. The Earth is suffering from a severe shortage of resources. Drought and famine occur regularly, and overpopulation has become an urgent issue. International space researchers have recently discovered a new planet, Zeta 4, which can be reached by human astronauts. Zeta 4 has plentiful supplies of water, and the atmosphere and climate appear to be ideal for human life. Our observations have also revealed that unknown life forms exist on the planet. You, as members of the space project committee, must now decide what action to take.

You must come to clear, convincing decisions on all of the following points:
a) whether you will remove any samples from Zeta 4 for laboratory analysis on Earth
b) an assessment of the likelihood of a friendly encounter with alien life forms
c) whether you would try to communicate with any life forms which might be encountered, and if so, what message you would try to transmit, and how
d) whether any astronauts who visit the planet should carry weapons
e) an assessment of the risk of damaging the natural environment on Zeta 4
f) whether you would make plans for the permanent human colonisation of Zeta 4.

Word list

Unit 8

allocate *v* [T] (86) to give money, time, space, etc. to be used for a particular purpose

astronomer *n* [C] (89) someone who scientifically studies stars and planets

astronomy *n* [U] (85) the scientific study of stars and planets

build a picture of something *phrase* (86) to gain an understanding of something

chiefly *adv* (85) mainly

comet *n* [C] (86) an object in space that leaves a bright line behind it in the sky

continuity *n* [U] (87) the state of continuing for a long period of time without changing or being stopped

cult following *np* [C] (RS) a group of people who very much like a particular thing that most people do not know about

distract someone from something *vp* [T] (85) to take someone's attention away from something

divert something from something *vp* [T] (85) to take someone's attention away from something

domain *n* [C] (85) a particular subject or activity that someone controls or deals with

early/ancient/modern, etc. civilisations *plural n* (85) the cultures and ways of life of societies at particular times

the end result *singular n* (RS) the result of an activity

evolve *v* [I/T] (86) to develop

for the purpose(s) of something *phrase* (85) in order to do something

found *v* [T] (85) to start an organisation, especially by providing money

galaxy *n* [C] (RS) a very large group of stars held together in the universe

geologist *n* [C] (86) someone who studies rocks and soil and the physical structure of the Earth

gravitational force *np* [U] (RS) the force that makes objects fall to the ground or that pulls objects towards a planet or other body

in collaboration with someone *phrase* (85) working together with someone

in the sense that *phrase* (85) in the way of thinking that

in turn *phrase* (92) as a result

intrinsic merit *np* [U] (85) If something has intrinsic merit, it has qualities itself.

introspective *adj* (85) thinking a lot about your own thoughts and feelings and not communicating these to other people

launch *n* [C] (88) the sending of a spacecraft into the sky

lens *n* [C] (RS) a curved piece of glass in cameras, glasses and scientific equipment used for looking at things

magnify *v* [T] (RS) to make an object look larger than it is by looking through special equipment

make a contribution to something *phrase* (85) to do something that helps something to develop or succeed

means *n* [C] (92) a way of doing something

minimise *v* [T] (87) to reduce something to the least amount or level

needless to say *phrase* (RS) as you would expect

obsessed with someone/something *adj* (RS) extremely interested in something

physiological *adj* (86) relating to how the bodies of living things work

primarily *adv* (85) mainly

realise *v* [T] (85) to achieve something

solar eclipse *np* [C] (RS) an occasion when the Moon passes between the Sun and the Earth, and the Moon blocks the light from the Sun

the solar system *singular n* (86) the sun and planets that move around it

sustain *v* [T] (RS) to allow something to continue

it is not uncommon for *phrase* (85) If you say it is not uncommon for something to happen, you mean it quite often happens.

undertake *v* [T] (86) to be responsible for a project or task that will take a long time or be difficult

the universe *singular n* (84) everything that exists, including stars, space, etc.

want nothing more than *phrase* (RS) to want most of all to do something

Vocabulary extension

Unit 8

automation *n* [U] when something is controlled using machines and not people, or the process of changing the control of something from people to machines

behave like a robot *vp* to function in the way that a robot functions

black hole *np* [C] an area in outer space that sucks material and light into it and from which it cannot escape

the cosmos *singular n* the whole universe

cyberspace *n* [U] the Internet, considered as an imaginary area where you can communicate with people and find information

a new / another dimension *phrase* a new/different aspect of a situation

experience the full force of something *vp* to experience something when it is at its most extreme

explosive sound *np* [C] the loud sound of something exploding

extraterrestrial *adj* coming from outside planet Earth

from a different perspective *np* If you consider a situation from a different perspective, you think about it in a different way.

in orbit *phrase* If a spacecraft or planet is in orbit, it is making a circular journey around a large object, such as another planet.

infinite number *phrase* a number which is so large that it is impossible to state or calculate

intelligent life *np* [U] living things that are able to understand and learn

interstellar *adj* between the stars

lunar *adj* relating to the moon

malfunction *v* [I] to fail to work or operate correctly

mission to explore *phrase* a flight into space with the aim of travelling around in order to learn about it

on board *phrase* on a boat, train, aircraft, spacecraft, etc.

over the moon *phrase* If someone is over the moon, they are very pleased about something that has happened.

planetary *adj* relating to planets

popularise *v* [T] to have the effect of making something liked by many people or known and understood by many people

prototype *n* [C] the first model or example of something new that can be developed or copied in the future

remote-controlled *adj* controlled from a distance, using a piece of equipment

rocket launch *np* [C] the sending into space of a rocket

seal *v* [T] to close an entrance or container so that air or liquid cannot enter or leave it

space shuttle *np* [C] a vehicle in which people travel into space and back again

space program(me) *np* [C] a plan of activities with the aim of sending vehicles and people into space

spur someone into action *vp* If something spurs you into action, it encourages you to do something, often in order to deal with a problem.

submersible *n* [C] a ship which can travel under water, especially one which operates with no people in it

unidentified flying object (UFO) *np* [C] something strange seen flying in the sky and thought by some people to be a spacecraft from a planet that is not Earth

unmanned *adj* A vehicle or machine that is unmanned has no people there to operate it.

vacuum *n* [C] a space that has no air or other gas in it

worth exploring *phrase* If something is worth exploring, there is a good reason for going there and finding out about it because it is important or interesting.

❶ **Match a verb from Box A with the rest of the phrase or idiom from Box B. Then complete the sentences below with the full phrase or idiom.**

A	bear	crack	make
	put	raise	read	~~take~~

B	awareness	down on	in mind	~~into account~~
	it down to experience	the most of	up on

0 In analysing the results of the survey, we should *take into account* take into account that most people actually do far less for the environment than they say they do.

1 The campaign aims to .... of endangered species.

2 Please .... that this is a nature reserve and do not leave any litter!

3 I found it very difficult to work with him, but will try to .... and learn from it!

4 The government says it is going to .... the big polluters.

5 You should .... the scenery while you can – they're building houses here next year.

6 I think my knowledge about climate change may be a bit outdated, I need to .... it.

❷ **Complete each of the sentences below using one word/phrase from the box.**

~~cultivate~~	diversity	fauna	longevity	monocrops	toxic	under threat

0 Organic farmers believe it is unnecessary to use pesticides to ....*cultivate*.... crops.

1 The .... of animals in the Amazon is incredible. There are hundreds of different species.

2 Every region has its own distinct flora and ....

3 Many pesticides and fungicides are .... to wildlife.

4 Much of the Amazon is being replaced with huge .... , such as soya and coffee.

5 While not yet critically endangered, the honey bee is certainly ....

6 It has been shown that the bees' health and .... is being affected by pesticides.

❸ **Complete this text by writing the correct preposition (*by, for, with, to,* etc.) in each gap.**

Space travel is usually regarded **(0)** ....*as*.... nothing more than a dream for the ordinary person. However, the entrepreneur, Richard Branson, has always believed **(1)** .... thinking outside the box and, as a result, he is currently devoting a lot of time and money **(2)** .... changing this perception.

In the Mojave desert, a group of engineers is currently involved **(3)** .... developing a spacecraft which aims to provide thousands of people **(4)** .... this opportunity within a few years.

No one will be prevented **(5)** .... flying, provided they agree **(6)** .... a medical exam – and can afford to pay $2,000 for a ticket!

❹ **Choose the correct option in italics for each gap.**

0 The President went to Cape Canaveral to see the rocket *lunch /(launch)*.

1 The *astrologer / astronomer* predicted a good month ahead for everyone born in June.

2 There are probably thousands of galaxies in our *universe / solar system*.

3 A rocket has to go very fast to break through the *Earth's gravitational force / solar system*.

4 The Moon went in front of the Sun causing a *solar system / solar eclipse*.

5 A *rocket / satellite* is designed to orbit a planet or other object in space.

6 Some people think that *galaxies / comets* may have originally brought life to Earth.

❺ **Choose TWO correct options in italics for each gap.**

There is (0) *little* / *any* / *no* doubt that the last few decades have devastated many of the world's natural landscapes. But, say botanical experts, there's every (1) *likelihood* / *chance* / *option* that this process can be at least partly reversed. These experts are planning a 20-year project to rescue these habitats, which is (2) *bound* / *likely* / *possible* to make a significant difference, even if it's highly (3) *probable* / *improbable* / *unlikely* that they can save them all.

It's very (4) *probable* / *likely* / *doubt* that funding will be found to save forests in Peru and Kenya, and there's (5) *a heavy likelihood* / *a fair chance* / *a strong possibility* that British wetlands will also be included in the project.

❻ **In each of these sentences, there is either a missing comma or a comma used incorrectly. Find and correct the mistakes.**

0 Northern Spain, where temperatures are still as low as 4°C, could see snow on the mountains.

1 In Florida Georgia and Alabama, temperatures could be unusually low, around 10°C.

2 Although, the weather is colder than average for the time of year, it will become gradually warmer over the next few days.

3 However, the forecast for the weekend is looking colder again with some rainfall and temperatures of just 14°C.

4 In Moscow, warm weather, which is still below average for the time of year will continue for another two or three days.

5 Wind across the Atlantic known as the jet stream, is part of the reason for the unsettled weather in northern Europe.

6 It is creating a block of low pressure, while southern Europe, is experiencing a heatwave.

❼ **Choose the correct option (A, B, C or D) to complete each sentence.**

0 What the space programme ....B......... restore confidence in the country.
   A was to   **B** did was to   **C** was to did   **D** did was

1 .... the cost of space tourism which makes it impractical.
   A What is   **B** What makes   **C** It is   **D** Which is

2 All that is required .... the government to commit more money to the space programme.
   A for   **B** which   **C** is that   **D** is for

3 What the report concluded .... ordinary people would never be able to afford space tourism.
   A that was   **B** that   **C** was that   **D** was

4 .... people don't consider is the environmental impact.
   A What   **B** That   **C** Is what   **D** What is

5 .... the space programme has been so expensive, the government is now cutting back.
   A What   **B** Whether   **C** Is   **D** Because

Answers

Progress tests

PROGRESS TEST Units 1–2

1 1 My most favourite subject on this course is marketing.
2 Physics is one of my least favourite subjects.
3 The greatest/highest number of complaints came from students in the business school.
4 He is one of the most cleverest students in my year.
5 It is often students in their first year who do the least amount of study.
6 Learning to be independent is the one of the most important things I learnt at university.

2 1 apparently   2 Generally speaking
3 arguably   4 Understandably   5 actually

3 1 pointed out   2 narrow down   3 back it up
4 work out   5 note them down   6 end up

4 1 for   2 in   3 with   4 to/for   5 with/against   6 for

5 1 a   2 The   3 –   4 –   5 a   6 The

6 1 A   2 C   3 C   4 A   5 B

7 1 have shown   2 has been   3 took place
4 had fallen / fell   5 rose   6 reached

PROGRESS TEST Units 3–4

1 1 factor   2 medicine   3 healing
4 condition   5 treatment   6 success

2 1 rate   2 types   3 amount
4 proportion   5 aspect   6 incidence

3 1 made   2 done   3 taken   4 takes/has   5 had   6 has

4 1 C   2 B   3 B   4 A   5 C

5 1 higher   2 slightly   3 almost
4 twice   5 lower   6 third   7 far

6 1 aim of drawing   2 owing to   3 consequence of inheriting   4 so (that) he can / so (that) he is able
5 with the result

7 1 large   2 rule   3 liable   4 tend   5 claimed

PROGRESS TEST Units 5–6

1 1 maintained links with
2 reached the point where
3 saved the day
4 turn the clock back
5 keep themselves to themselves
6 broken new ground

2 1 unstable/destabilised
2 underestimated/overestimated   3 inhospitable
4 decelerate   5 illogical   6 worthless

3 1 to/for   2 over   3 of   4 from   5 to

4 1 noteworthy   2 detrimental   3 huge
4 instant   5 large   6 integral

5 1 wouldn't have   2 would never have found
3 didn't have   4 unless   5 hadn't seen
6 Had we had

6 1 this/that   2 so/it   3 This/That
4 one/them   5 neither   6 It/This

7 1 Two thousand years ago, the Romans invaded large parts of the world, influencing many aspects of life.
2 The writing in some of these documents is very unclear, making it difficult to read.
3 Even in ancient times, Homo sapiens travelled great distances, enabling them to buy, sell and exchange useful materials.
4 During the medieval period many castles were built, protecting the land from enemies.
5 The ancient Greeks influenced many areas of life, including science, politics, philosophy and the arts.

PROGRESS TEST Units 7–8

1 1 raise awareness   2 bear in mind
3 put it down to experience   4 crack down on
5 make the most of   6 read up on

2 1 diversity   2 fauna   3 toxic
4 monocrops   5 under threat   6 longevity

3 1 in   2 to   3 in   4 with   5 from   6 to

4 1 astrologer   2 universe   3 gravitational force
4 solar eclipse   5 satellite   6 comets

5 1 likelihood; chance   2 bound; likely
3 improbable; unlikely   4 probable; likely
5 a fair chance; a strong possibility

6 1 comma needed after Florida
2 no comma after Although
3 comma needed after again
4 comma needed after year
5 comma needed after Atlantic
6 no comma after Europe

7 1 C   2 D   3 C   4 A   5 D

Speaking reference

Part 1 Topics and questions

❶ 1 f 2 j 3 l 4 a 5 k 6 d 7 g
8 b 9 i 10 c 11 h 12 e

❷ *Suggested answers*

1 You have to think about the impact it can have on people around you …

2 Well, I've always dreamed of working in the catering industry, but now I think I'd do better in the field of education because …

3 Horses and camels are an integral part of life in my country. They …

4 We played a wide range of sports, such as ….

5 It's a very ancient city, and one of its outstanding features is a clock tower that is …

6 When I'm free, I prefer to see my friends, although I also think it's important to take an interest in family life …

7 Most of my birthdays were spent at my grandmother's home. I used to receive a huge number of presents, which …

8 I really enjoy going to museums and looking at old clothes and fashion items, and one of the key aspects for me is imagining the people who wore them …

9 I feel stressed! What I try to do is to make a decision about what to do first – what's most crucial – and then stick to it!

10 We didn't get many opportunities to do art when I was a primary school student because …

11 I much prefer them to be light and I also like my windows to face the sun so that I can make the most of the daylight.

12 I'm not sure, actually. It would be exciting to be able to take advantage of all the perks that celebrities get, but I wouldn't want to have the paparazzi following me everywhere.

How are you rated?

1 b, e
2 d, g
3 a, h
4 c, f

Writing reference

Task 1

1 Graphs that compare figures at different points in time

❶ 1 The percentage of the population that is over 60
2 Two periods: 2000 and 2050
3 They are the figures for the world; the rest of the figures are subsumed in these.
4 The high figures for Europe in both years; the growth in the ageing population across the world; the particularly strong growth in Asia, Latin America and Africa
5 Past simple tense for 2000; future tenses and passive forms for 2050

❷ 1 Overall, the proportions around the world are predicted to rise significantly. / In 2000, Europe had the largest group of ageing citizens, at 20 percent of its population. / … the biggest increases in this age group, relative to the rest of the population, are predicted to occur in Asia, Latin America and Africa.

2 more than double; rise more in some parts of the world than in others; the largest group; The second-largest group; by far the greatest percentage; the biggest increases; increase almost threefold; more than double; much more significant

3 is likely to change; are predicted to rise; this will more than double; is expected to rise; is still going to have; figures likely to reach; are predicted to occur; will increase; will more than double; will maintain; will be much more significant

2 Charts/tables/graphs that show related information

❶ 1 They are both about UK graduates and employment. The table gives employment figures, while the pie charts look at salaries among the employed group.

2 The similarities across the four years in the table; the level of employment compared to other activities; the peak in salaries of women in the $20,000–$24,999 bracket; the fact that women earn more than men up to $25,000 per annum and less after this

3 *Suggested answer*: Describe the table first, as this is more general and global. Then describe the charts, as they relate to one row in the table.

❷ 1 According to the table, the pattern in graduate destinations altered very little over this period.

2 The overview is the final paragraph.

❸ 1 altered very little   2 category   3 opted for
4 approximately   5 the majority   6 levels
7 secured jobs

3 Graphs that show trends over time

❶ 1 The overall trend, which fluctuates and declines;
the significant fall in cases between 1955 and
1975; the peaks around 1980 and subsequent fall
2 The difference in the number of cases prior to
and during vaccination; the opposing trends in
vaccination uptake and number of cases
3 The direct link between the number of cases and
the uptake of vaccination

❷ 1 Paragraph 1: introduction and overview;
paragraph 2: the overall trend up to the
introduction of a vaccine; paragraph 3: the trend
in the uptake of the vaccine and how this affected
the number of cases
2 In the first paragraph, after the introduction
3 Figures are included for the overall trend and to
support the key features on the graph.

❸ 1 However; Although   2 Overall; until; Following
this; until; gradually   3 resulted in; as

4 Diagrams that show a process and/or how something works

❶ 1 Preparing the land and planting; pruning and
thinning; felling and transporting to mills
2 *Suggested answers*: Saplings (young trees); tractor;
machinery; by hand; cut down; electric saw; lorry;
transport; made into
3 *Suggested answers*: the different uses of trees; the
different points at which trees are cut down; the
use of machinery and manpower
4 *Suggested answer*: The fact that the different stages
impact in different ways on the life cycle of the
trees

❷ Before; Once; Over time; As; at this stage; until;
When this happens; Meanwhile

❸ the land must be cleared and prepared; Heavy
machinery is used; Once this has been done; saplings
that have been grown … are taken … and planted;
they are pruned by hand; the forest is thinned; Trees
that have been cut down … are used for firewood;
are not removed; until they are required; are felled
… and prepared; The trunks are transported; they
are turned; they are dried and cut; to be used;
is prepared; the agricultural process required to
produce; are cut down; are planted

Task 2

1 To what extent do you agree?

❶ b

❷ 2 parents   3 jobs   4 career ladder   5 natural
progression   6 economic climate   7 decision   8 plan

❸ 1 The first consideration; So the second consideration
2 On the other hand

❹ 1 secure suitable employment   2 fund their studies
3 have no real desire to   4 start at the bottom
5 enter a certain profession

❺ **go round** – to be enough for everyone in a group of
people; **work your way up** – gradually do more of an
activity until you reach a particular level; **carry on** –
continue doing; **turn out** – to happen in a particular
way or have a particular result

2 Benefits and drawbacks

❶ 1 Technological tools have enhanced safety and
security versus loss of privacy.

❷ *Suggested answer*: Technology has made people's lives
safer and reduced their anxiety, but we still need to
make sure that it is never used in inappropriate ways.

❸ it is inevitable that; what is important is how;
I believe that; No one can deny that; Like CCTV; it is
true that; It is perfectly possible that; it is up to us to
ensure that; that does not mean that

❹ **they** – new devices; **This type of surveillance** –
the public being monitored on the platforms; **this
concern** – being nervous about flying; **it** – the process
of being scanned; **this** – the fact that new inventions
are criticised; **Such uses** – misusing data or passing
it on to other organisations; **this is what happens** –
technology is used wisely; **that** – technology being
used wisely and people complaining only because
they are impatient or short-sighted

3 Two questions

❶ 1 **this** – human activity being the greatest threat to
plant and animal life
2 *Suggested answers*: Why it has happened: habitat
loss / building and deforestation / species
extinction / hunting / population growth / global
warming
How we can reduce it: protecting species /
charitable work / government initiatives /
sustainable building / limit urban growth / reduce
activities that contribute to global warming /
international collaboration

② Paragraphs 2 and 3 deal with the first question: *One of the main reasons why / another contributing factor* Paragraphs 4 and 5 deal with the second question: *As individuals / What governments need to do*

③ it is this sense of harmony with nature; An inevitable result has been; What governments need to do

④ **recapture** – get back; **shift** – change; **have taken their toll** – have caused suffering or damage; **tackled** – dealt with; **collaborate** – work together; **redress the situation** – put the situation right

Practice test

Listening, Section 1

1 23rd July / 23/7 / 7/23
2 HEPWORTH
3 07968 355630
4 electric(ity)
5 drain/sewer
6 SEW 47
7 (swimming) pool
8 laundry
9 litter/rubbish
10 shower/washroom key

Narrator: You will hear a woman talking on the phone to a campsite manager.

Man: Hi, Lake Pane Campground. Can I help you?

Woman: Oh, hi, yes, um, I wonder if we could book a site on your campground?

M: Sure. My computer's down at the moment, so I just need to get a form. OK – how many nights would you like to stay for?

W: Um, well, ideally, we'd like to stay for five.

M: Five nights, OK.

(pause)

Man: Hi, Lake Pane Campground. Can I help you?

Woman: Oh, hi, yes, um, I wonder if we could book a site on your campground?

M: Sure. My computer's down at the moment, so I just need to get a form. OK – how many nights would you like to stay for?

W: Um, well, ideally, we'd like to stay for five.

M: Five nights, OK. So when are you planning to arrive?

W: Well, we'll be travelling around the area from mid-July and we think we'll be at the lake by about the 24th.

M: Let's see. July's a busy time. We could probably fit you in, but to be honest, if you want five nights, it would be better to get here a day earlier. We've got a big group coming at the end of the month.

W: OK – the 23rd's fine. We weren't sure so …

M: Great. Do you just want somewhere to park and pitch a tent, or do you have an RV?

W: An RV?

M: Yeah – you know, a recreational vehicle … a campervan.

W: Oh, right – yes, we're driving a van, so …

M: OK – that's fine. So, um, what name is it, please?

W: It's Hepworth, that's H-E-P-W-O-R-T-H.

M: OK, thanks. I've heard that name before.

W: Well, it's quite common in England – particularly in Yorkshire. That's where we're from.

M: I was going to ask you that. It's a really good line, isn't it?

W: Yes.

M: Would this be your contact number?

W: Yes – it's 07968 355630.

M: Great, thanks.

W: Do you want my home number as well?

M: No – that's fine.

W: OK.

M: We supply a number of facilities. I don't know if you're familiar with the way campgrounds work here.

W: It would be good if you could explain.

M: Well, you're coming in the RV, so would you like to hook up to our electricity?

W: Oh, yes, please.

M: You can also attach your vehicle to the water taps here.

W: I hope it's all easy to do!

M: Yeah – you just plug into the electric and switch on the water. The people who hire out the RVs will explain it all.

W: OK – and what about waste water?

M: Sure – you can have a site with a sewer – or I think you guys call it a drain – that's a bit extra. Not all campgrounds have that facility, you see.

W: Fine, we'll have it. So what's the total and …

(pause)

M: OK – I've allocated you a site, so you need to note the code down.

W: Right, I'll just get a pen.

M: Most of our sites are coded using letters and numbers … EW or SEW.

W: Uh-huh.

M: So yours is one of the SEW ones and it's number 47.

W: Got that.

M: That's the area that has all the requirements you need.

W: Is it easy to find when you get there?

M: What time will you be arriving?

W: I'm not sure, but it could be quite late.

M: OK, so the reception could be closed. We close at six.

W: Oh dear.

M: It's OK – I'll tell you where to go. As you come in the campground entrance, you'll see our office.

W: Uh-huh.

M: Drive past the front door … there's another office next to ours, that's the business office. Yeah, and there's a pool behind that.

W: OK – it would be good to have a swim!

M: It's open till eight, so feel free to use it. Keep going past all those … to the end of the track. At the top, you'll come to a … at the very end there's a laundry.

W: OK.

M: Turn left at the laundry and you'll see your own site straight ahead of you. They're all clearly labelled.

W: That sounds easy enough.

M: Just before you hang up … um … we've had a few problems with campers … with, um, stuff left lying around.

W: Oh!

M: Well, it may be an oversight, but we do ask our visitors to take away all their litter.

W: Of course. Otherwise someone has to clear it up!

M: That's right. Also, in the morning … you know … we do have washrooms, and once the reception's open, you'll be able to get a key for the shower.

W: Right.

M: You can keep it while you're on the site, but could you return it when you leave?

W: I'll make sure we get it back to you.

M: Yeah – otherwise we don't have enough to go around.

W: OK – well, thank you very much. See you soon!

M: Yeah – bye.

Section 2

11 E
12 A
13 D
14 F
15 B
16 C
17 A
18 packaging
19 environment
20 creative

Narrator: You will hear someone talking on the radio about colours.

Presenter: Well it's a 'colourful' start to the day on DB Radio. Kathy, what have you got to tell us?

Kathy: Thanks, Briony. I thought I'd talk about two areas today where colour plays a huge role in our lives – and they are food and fashion. So, let's start with food and more specifically, food colouring.

In many parts of the world today, people like the food they purchase to be the 'right' colour. So if we buy tinned or canned vegetables, such as green peas, it's highly likely that the contents have been enhanced through the use of colouring agents. Peas are naturally green, you might say. But they may not be green all over or they may not be the most pleasing shade of green. So a natural additive or two can quickly sort that out, just as it can the perfectly minty green ice cream that we buy our children.

Children are a big market for food and are easily tempted by colour. Breakfast cereals, for instance, that come in various shades of brown are often altered using caramel, a natural brown food colouring derived from caramelised sugar. This also gives the cereals a shiny, mouth-watering appeal which is hugely tempting for consumers.

In fact, natural food colouring goes back a long way. One of the oldest – or perhaps the most well-known natural food colours – is red or 'cochineal', named after the insects used to make it. Aztec Indians created a crimson dye from the bodies of crushed beetles. Producing cochineal is very costly, so it was unpopular with consumers for some years. But health scares linking artificial red dyes to cancer have meant that more shoppers are buying cochineal again.

Now, there's one food colour that manufacturers use with a certain amount of caution and that's blue. Our ancestors believed that food this colour was dangerous. If you think about it, very few naturally occurring foods are blue, and there is little demand for the colouring. In fact, if you're trying to lose weight, experts suggest that you put your food on a blue plate. It's almost guaranteed to kill your appetite.

(pause)

OK, let's look at another area where colour is a key issue. If you say you've bought something new to wear, often the first question people will ask is 'What colour is it?' Yet the answer doesn't necessarily indicate that the colour was your preferred choice. As consumers, we have to balance how we feel in certain colours with what is fashionable at the time. You think you've suddenly developed a desire to wear orange, whereas, in fact, the shops are full of it, and you've ended up buying an orange shirt – that may or may not suit you – simply because it's 'this season's colour'.

Well, the interesting thing here is that 'colourists', as they're called in the business, have to look ahead and say what colour models will be wearing in fashion shows several years in advance. To get this right, they have to consider how long it will take to produce the cloth dyes, they have to set up deals with suppliers, and bear in mind the constant changes in consumer taste. So what may seem to be this season's colour has actually been agreed years before.

So what do we think about the colours we wear? Like everything, our tastes alter with age. In general, though, we think that black makes people look and feel thinner, while red does the opposite; white goes with everything, whereas yellow is harder to match, and nothing alters the fact that there are certain colours that we never feel comfortable wearing.

And finally – whether it's food or fashion, anyone in the business field knows that it isn't enough to get a product the right colour. Even the packaging has to be carefully designed in order to maximise sales. It's no good, for instance, wrapping an item in brown paper if you want it to stand out. Much better to go for eye-catching colours or, in fact, in today's world, green has become very popular because it promotes the view that the company cares about the environment. In addition to their products, businesses also have to think about the people who come up with the ideas. If you surround your workers with drab colours, they'll come up with equally dull ideas. This isn't rocket science. We used to associate red with creativity in business, but it turns out – according to a recent study – that blue is a much better stimulus for creative thought. So the colour's not all bad!

Section 3

21 definition
22 breakdown
23 private/Private
24 Europe
25 destinations
26 competition/opportunities
27/28 B, E
29/30 B, D

Narrator: You will hear a tutor and two students discussing international mobility.

Tutor: Hi Nils, hi Eva. Come in and sit down. You wanted to talk about your research paper, is that right?

Nils: Yes, we've drawn up an outline for the introduction and done some preliminary interviews.

T: And how did that go?

Eva: We've come across some interesting findings.

T: OK – let's go through what you've done so far. What's the subject?

N: Right, so we're doing our paper on international student mobility.

E: We're looking at the overall picture, you know where overseas students are going in the world to study and why … and we think that picture's changing.

T: Sounds interesting.

E: The first thing we've looked at is numbers, and as part of that, er, how many students there are in total who are studying outside their own country …

N: That *seems* easy. It looks like it's around three million.

E: However, the definition of the term 'international student' varies across countries.

N: Yeah, and because of that, the figure *could* be much higher.

T: I see.

E: Then we looked at different countries – we wanted to know what the breakdown of numbers is around the world, you know, how many students go where. But we're not sure how accurate those figures are either.

N: Yeah, even though it's the fastest-growing sector of higher education, some ministries don't include the students at private institutions in their count.

E: It's quite frustrating. Anyway, next we wanted to know where the majority of students come from.

N: This is something that's changing quite rapidly.

T: Well, that would be an interesting point. What's changing?

E: Most people know that the largest group of international students comes from East Asia.

N: But what we hadn't realised is that figures for the US have quadrupled over the past 20 years, and a lot more students from Europe are also now studying abroad.

T: Ah-hah.

N: Yeah – we need to look at some more figures there.

E: Lastly, we looked at the countries that students go to – and the trends there.

N: Yeah, our question really was about the destinations of international students and whether they're changing.

E: And they are! Countries like China are providing more higher education opportunities for their own students and for students from places like Britain.

N: This means that higher education is becoming more – well, there are high levels of competition.

E: But with that there's also a spirit of exchange – it's not so one-sided any more.

(pause)

T: So you said you'd done some preliminary interviews?

E: Yes – we thought we'd start by talking to some of the international students in our city.

N: Just to help us design the web interviews we plan to do.

T: OK.

E: We wanted to find out if there are common factors that students consider to be important when they choose an overseas course.

N: Obviously, these will vary across the international student population, but we thought some, like cost, might be significant.

E: Surprisingly, a lot of students said they left finances to their parents, but they did want to know that their university was a good one.

N: They said they decided about this by talking to friends at home – not by looking at how many degrees or publications the staff had.

E: That's right. But they *were* interested in the *degrees* they were taking and whether when they finished their course they'd get a good job.

N: I'm not sure I would have given the same answers, but …

T: OK. What else did you ask them about?

N: What sort of incentives they think source countries should offer students – to encourage them to return home after they've graduated.

T: A very interesting question. What did you find?

E: Well, many said that if they chose to get another qualification, they'd stay or move to a third country to do this.

N: Yeah, so there doesn't seem to be much point in offering scholarships to get them to return home to study.

T: What about grants for research?

N: Post-graduation, that was much more popular, especially if the system let them compete individually for these.

E: And many students were keen to go home and get a job if they could be sure they'd have a good income and lifestyle.

N: For example, they felt that the government should perhaps offer tax exemptions so that they could afford to live in a nice area.

T: Some countries have created special work zones for incoming graduates, particularly in the science field.

N: Yeah and some of these include apartment blocks as well.

E: Mmm. But as many of the students we talked to were Arts students, this didn't seem to appeal to them.

T: OK, well, I think that's a pretty good start, let's just …

Section 4

31 forest
32 Australia
33 clothing
34 Fossil evidence
35 (is) unknown
36 human hair
37 protection
38 toys / toy lions / models / model lions
39 Long dark / Dark long
40 status symbol

Narrator: You will hear a lecture on lions.

Lecturer: As part of this series of lectures on wildlife, I'm going to talk today about lions, about their history and about some of the work that's been done with lions in recent years.

When we think of lions, we tend to think of Africa, as this is the only area of the world where they still exist in the wild, apart from some small groups in the Indian forest of Gir. But you might be surprised to know that lions were once virtually everywhere on the planet. In fact, if you go back 500,000 years, there were more lions roaming the world than dogs or monkeys. You could bump into one in London, Moscow or LA, in every part of Africa, apart from the desert; in fact, the only continents that were and have always been lion-free were the frozen plains of Antarctica – which were obviously much too inhospitable for this jungle creature – and Australia, though there is plenty of bushland there.

So what happened? Well, we know for certain that as recently as the 1800s – that's just 200 years ago – lions were being hunted to extinction in some parts of the world, sometimes just for sport. But long before that, about 10,000 years ago, lions started to disappear from various corners of the globe. Scientists believe there was the usual battle with our human ancestors for food, in the form of other, smaller creatures, with many lions also being killed to make clothing.

So lions may have gone from Europe, but there are plenty of prehistoric paintings to witness their presence. And they reveal some interesting facts.

Let's take a look … These cave paintings were found in France – the outlines are slightly blurred because they were hand-drawn using materials like charcoal or ochre. But the images are still very clear and the interesting thing is that, as you can see, in the past, lions were actually a lot bigger than they are now – they come up to this man's waist! You may think the size has been exaggerated because of the man's fear, but there's plenty of fossil evidence that supports the larger proportions these animals once had, when you compare them with the African lions of the present day. The other curious thing here is that none of the male lions seen in cave paintings like this have the long, black or blond hair around their necks and faces that is called a mane. Now, the lion's mane is another interesting feature of these creatures. No one seems to know much about it – there are none in cave paintings like these – and, even today, the date when the lion's mane first appeared is unknown, and there is disagreement among scientists as to what its purpose is.

A lot of work has gone into researching this. If you think about it, no other cat has a mane. So why does a lion have one? And a lion's mane can be various lengths and colours, not unlike human hair: some are long, some are short; they can be black, brown or blond and they can be in good or bad condition. What scientists do know is that when lions fight, they tend to go for each other's necks and, at first, this led

some researchers to believe that the mane acts as a form of protection during battles with neighbouring prides. That may be partly true. But not everyone agrees it's the whole explanation. One leading lion expert believes that manes are more to do with attracting females and scaring off males, and he's run an experiment to test this theory out.

What he did was to make five toy lions and put them in the lions' territory. He made sure they all looked different – some had long, light-coloured manes, some had short, dark ones and so on. He put these in places where they were sure to be seen, and for a while the lions ignored them. But eventually they went up to the models. And, well, the female lions were attracted to the ones that had long, dark manes. The male lions weren't, they just kept away from them – what interested them were the ones with short, blond manes. They approached these and bit or clawed them quite aggressively.

When the results of this study were compared with the real-world situation, it was found that lions with long, dark manes tend to be the healthiest, while ones with short, blond manes are more likely to be injured or sick. Thus, the team concluded that a lion's mane is effectively a status symbol; that it shows how strong and healthy the lion is and, as a result, makes the lion more attractive to females.

Reading

Section 1

1 FALSE
2 TRUE
3 NOT GIVEN
4 TRUE
5 NOT GIVEN
6 FALSE
7 three/3 metres (high)
8 (bird-like) beak
9 curved claws
10 asymmetrical vanes
11 (at) dusk
12 southern/warmer
13 food chain

Section 2

14 C   15 G   16 D   17 B   18 F   19 D   20 B   21 C
22 B   23 A   24 Hirschfeld attributes
25 automated system   26 exaggerated

Section 3

27 NOT GIVEN   28 YES   29 NO   30 NO
31 NOT GIVEN   32 YES   33 F   34 C   35 A   36
E   37 D   38 B   39 B   40 A

Writing

Task 1

> **Sample answer**
>
> The graph shows the rapidly growing number of 3D cinema screens around the world, while the chart provides information on two types of film that are released in 3D, and shows how their relative numbers have changed over time.
>
> Clearly, the global increase in 3D screens has been significant. In 2005, there were none, and initially the increase in numbers was minimal. However, between 2008 and 2011, there was a steep rise to just over 35,000 screens, after which numbers seemed to flatten out a little.
>
> The chart shows a similar pattern in terms of 3D film releases. Very few animated films and no live-action films existed in this format up to 2007. In 2008, live action and animated films were released in equally small numbers. However, between 2009 and 2012, the combined number of these films increased dramatically to about 75. In addition, the number of live-action films grew faster, so that by this date there were twice as many live-action films as animations.
>
> To summarise, there has evidently been significant growth in 3D cinema, with the number of live-action 3D films outstripping that of animations by the end of the period covered in the data.

Task 2

> **Sample answer**
>
> Most people are aware that they need to take some responsibility for their health by eating sensibly and taking regular exercise, and many succeed in doing this. The reasons why others fail can be complex and do not necessarily mean that they rely on the medical profession to keep them healthy.
>
> The main reasons people give for being less healthy than others are often economic. People who fail to eat sensibly argue that they do not have the time or the money to cook nutritious meals. Being busy and working long hours also affect people's willingness to give up time to go to the gym or join a sports club. These may seem valid excuses, but ultimately they can lead to a sedentary lifestyle.
>
> These days, research has shown that there is a direct link between inactivity and illness. Eating large quantities of fat, for instance, can result in weight gain, which can lead to high blood pressure or arthritis; heart-related problems are common among people who live stressful, inactive lives. Eventually, people may end up requiring prescription drugs and hospital appointments in order to treat their conditions.
>
> It is often only after this has happened that people decide to change their diet and start exercising, usually on the advice of their doctor. Clearly, if they had always had a healthy lifestyle, they would not have needed medical treatment. However, once they do become ill, most people take steps to redress the situation as best they can.
>
> In summary, most people try, with varying degrees of success, to live a healthy lifestyle, even if they take some time to realise how important this is. Only a small proportion of the population are unable to change, and thus rely on doctors.

Acknowledgements

The authors and publishers are grateful to the following contributors:

Editors: Catriona Watson-Brown and Andrew Reid

Additional material: David Jay, Jo Preshous and Rachael Roberts

Lexicographer: Kate Woodford

Illustrations: Martin Sanders pp72, 114

Designed and typeset by Wild Apple Design Ltd

The authors and publishers acknowledge the following sources of photographs and are grateful for the permissions granted.

p. 16 (T): Sherrie Nickol/Citizen Stock/Corbis; p. 16 (C): Juanmonino/iStock; p. 16 (B): Francisco Romero/iStock.